MEMORIES

Esse
Ghosthunter

Wesley Downes

COUNTRYSIDE BOOKS
NEWBURY BERKSHIRE

Dedication

This book is dedicated to my late wife Peggy and to my family, who so patiently endured hour after hour listening to my incessant two-finger tapping and the prolonged time I spent at my desk completely oblivious of their very existence.

To them I can only say that I hope that the means have justified the ends or vice-versa.

Also I wish to express my sincere thanks to all who have helped me with this book, both with stories, information and suggestions.

Last, but certainly not least, a very big 'Thank You' to my good friend George, for his criticism, correcting and editing – a mammoth job well done.

First published 2009
© Wesley Downes 2009

COUNTRYSIDE BOOKS
3 Catherine Road
Newbury, Berkshire

To view our complete range of books,
please visit us at
www.countrysidebooks.co.uk

ISBN 978 1 84674 160 9

Cover picture supplied by Des Knock,
www.desknockphotography.co.uk

Designed by Peter Davies, Nautilus Design
Typeset by Mac Style, Beverley, E. Yorkshire
Produced through MRM Associates Ltd., Reading
Printed by Information Press

·Contents·

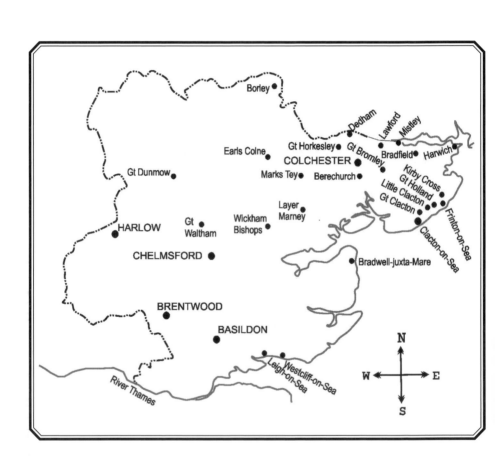

Contents

• Introduction •

Having a night out with a ghosthunter may sound very exciting to some, but to others the mere thought might perhaps send shivers down their backs, let alone make their hair stand on end. As one who has been a psychic investigator for over 60 years on and off, passing lonely nights *and* days in all sorts of weather, come rain, snow or shine and everything in between, I would hate to count the hours I have spent in the hope of getting just a glimpse of a ghost or even catching the sound of a hoarse, unaccountable whisper.

You may think that to be a ghosthunter you have to be slightly mad, after all, what sane person would try to prove what plain commonsense tells you does not exist. Nevertheless, there are thousands of like-minded people, of both sexes, throughout the world who devote much of their spare time doing just that!

Having on numerous occasions been asked how I became involved with the paranormal – and ghosthunting in particular – the answer is simple, it was literally by accident.

It all started way back in 1946 when, having been demobbed from the RAF, I was living with my parents at Ardleigh, near Colchester. Having been into town to do some shopping, I was cycling home through Parsons Heath when I saw a young man walking towards me on the opposite side of the road. As we drew nearer, I recognised him as a lad from my schooldays and, when opposite him, called out but he took no notice and carried on walking at a fair pace. Turning round and going back, I again called out but he continued to ignore me. Because by now I was quite close to him, I went to slap him on his shoulder but my hand went right through him and being off balance I fell off my bike. Picking myself up and somewhat shocked, I looked round for him, but he had completely vanished.

When I got home and told my mother what had happened, she said that she was certain my schoolfriend had been killed during the war and suggested that I should go and have a word with his mother, who still lived in the village. Later that afternoon I did as suggested and went to see Mrs B.... who was pleased to see me, but was shocked at what I had to say. She broke down in tears as she told me that her son had been 'missing, presumed killed' in the D-Day landings and this was the anniversary of that fateful day!

A few days later, the story was reported in the local press and was obviously read by a senior member of the Ghost Club who contacted me to verify my experience and invited me to attend a meeting to tell their members about it. I accepted the invitation and, after relating the incident and answering a few questions, I was invited to join the Club and had the pleasure of not only attending many of their meetings but also later becoming one of their investigators.

In the 1970s, there was a difference of opinion within the Club and, as a result, a new organisation – The Ghost Club Society – was formed and I was invited to become their Eastern Area Investigating Officer, a position that I held for many years.

Living in the Colchester and Clacton areas for more than 60 years, it was inevitable that I should become involved in investigating some of the many alleged paranormal incidents that have taken place in Essex and I hope the reader will enjoy reading about some of my experiences.

Wesley Downes

BASILDON

The Floating Monk

This account about an experience he had in 1971 was related to me by someone who used to live in Lynge Road, Basildon and worked for the nearby photographic company, Ilford Ltd. Late one summer Friday afternoon, his manager asked him if he would mind working until 6 o'clock that evening in order to complete an urgent order, to which he readily agreed. When the work was completed, he left the premises and started to cycle home along the main road until turning into what was locally known as 'the old road', which took him past Holy Cross church and churchyard.

Just before reaching the church, he noticed what he took to be a man dressed in clerical attire coming from the field opposite the church. Without looking in either direction, the figure walked straight across the road in front of him, so close in fact, that he almost ran into him.

The cleric appeared to be completely oblivious of the near accident and continued on his way into the churchyard. The following Sunday, after having attended the morning service, the cyclist had the opportunity to have a quiet word with the vicar and to politely admonish him for nearly causing an accident. However, the priest assured him it was definitely not him who had crossed the road at that time, but he thought that what he had seen could well have been the apparition of a monk who had been known to cross the road from the field about that time of the day, when he was apparently on his way back to his own grave in the churchyard!

What is even more remarkable is the fact that this particular monk's grave is on the north side of the church, the area normally unconsecrated and used mainly for suicides, witches, unbelievers and the like and sometimes referred to as the Devil's Acre. Although it is doubtful whether the truth will ever be known, one can only conjecture as to why a monk should have been buried there in the first place.

Some time later, the gentleman related his story to a lady colleague who told him that when one evening both she and a friend had been working late at the factory and were cycling home, they too saw what they took to be a monk appear from the field and cross the road ahead of them and vanish into a grave in the graveyard. They were so scared that neither of them went that way home again, preferring to take the far longer route!

Shortly after this, two young girls, while cycling along a road near the Ford motor factory, were startled to see what they were also convinced was a monk *floating* along the footpath coming from the churchyard, then cross the road and turn into the factory gates, where he vanished. No amount of questioning – and leg pulling – could make them change their story.

In 1973 a curate of Holy Cross church reported hearing strange and unaccountable sounds within his church and when looking round, caught a fleeting glimpse of what he took to be a monk just fading into what appeared to be a fine mist before vanishing altogether.

BERECHURCH

The Ghostly Horseman in the Sky

A family, then living in East Mersea in Essex, related the following strange story about their experience one afternoon in 1980.

They were on their way to visit a relative in a Colchester hospital – a distance of about eight miles – and, being locals, they knew the easiest and shortest route through the lanes to avoid the lengthy hold-ups due to major roadworks that were taking place along the main road. Turning off the Mersea road just past the Manwood Bridge, they followed what was then a winding lane that passed the old Berechurch church into Berechurch Hall Road near to the Military Corrective Training Centre (the army 'Glasshouse').

They were about halfway along the lane when they were surprised to see a grey shape loom up some fifty yards ahead. As they neared, this turned out to be a horse with a rider who could well have been a First World War soldier. He appeared to be looking straight ahead, and was obviously tall, sitting very upright in the saddle with his legs straight down in the stirrups. He was wearing a greyish uniform with a sash across his chest, which might have been a Sam Browne belt, and on his back was a large pack. His hat was of Australian style, turned up on the left-hand side and held in position by a badge of some sort. In his right hand he held a staff, which extended a couple of feet above his head and on the top of which was a triangular pennant being blown backwards by the wind. He was also holding the reins with his left hand, while hanging from his left side was a long sword.

The strangest thing of all was that this apparition appeared to be not only high in the air, jumping over trees and just under very low cloud, but the horse seemed to be at full gallop and just clearing the trees.

Shortly after this account was published in the *Ghosts and Hauntings* magazine, the editor received a letter from a Clacton-on-Sea reader saying that, having read the above story, he recalled that during the 1914–18 war, his grandfather used to supply horses that had not been 'broken in' to the army at Cherry Tree Camp, Colchester (near to where the incident was claimed to have taken place) and the description fitted the Australian 'rough-riders' who were stationed for a while at the camp.

These Australians consisted mostly of convicts (some of them murderers) who were given the opportunity to 'volunteer' their services in the war and in return (if they survived) their sentences would be taken as having been served.

BORLEY

The Ghosts, Myths and Legends of Borley Church

Publications regarding Essex ghosts would not be complete without at least a passing reference to Borley, a small village on the county border, between Sudbury and Long Melford. Over the years, this village has probably received more than its fair share of attention and publicity, most of it – according to some of the residents – unwanted, unwelcome and untrue.

The main attraction in the 1920s and 30s was the rectory, once described as 'the most haunted house in England'. Many books, numerous newspaper and magazine articles, all expressing varying points of view, have been written about the alleged hauntings there. However, after a disastrous fire in 1939 and the eventual demolition of the rectory in 1944, much more attention was given to the church and its churchyard, where even to this day strange things are said to happen.

On various occasions, coffins in the crypt of this 12th-century church have been found to have been moved and left poised at odd angles. These were, of course, put back in their original positions but, when next inspected were again found to be scattered about – how and by whom?

Another unsolved mystery concerns the church plate. According to legend, when in the 1640s Oliver Cromwell's men were plundering the churches, the wise clergy of Borley decided to bury most of the church valuables in the churchyard until better times. Because this was done at night and with the utmost secrecy, nobody appears to have made a note of just where they were buried and therefore the location still remains a mystery. Some years ago, a diviner, having tried – but failed – to find the treasure, nevertheless discovered what was thought could have been the remains of a tunnel running under the road from the church towards the site of the rectory.

With so much activity in the rectory, there is even more in and around the church, as can well be expected. This includes the sighting of a nun, seen many times in the churchyard by a number of people, and the ghost of what is believed to have been a teenaged girl dressed in blue, as well as a veiled woman near the church, although it is difficult to decide whether this veiled figure and that of the nun are one and the same.

Inside the church itself, there are areas reputed to have cold spots with a sensation of 'tension' around them. There is an account of a young boy who, while visiting the church with his parents and walking down the aisle, suddenly stood rigid as if frozen to the spot and stared straight ahead, wide-eyed. After what seemed to be ages, he suddenly burst into tears and ran out. When his parents eventually found him, he was hiding behind a yew tree in the churchyard, still crying his eyes out, and all they could get out of him was that 'it was so cold'!

Numerous visitors have stated that when walking along the path towards the church door they have heard organ music coming from within the church. In the late 1980s, an elderly lady and her 41-year-old daughter, after slowly making their way up the same path and hearing the organ being played with gusto and thinking that a practice was taking place, waited for a break in the music before opening the church door. They were somewhat surprised to find that not only was the organ locked, but there was no sign of an organist. Somewhat puzzled, they continued to look around and admire the church and were about to leave when they were showered with what appeared to be small pebbles from above. Not only could they not see anyone but, much to their surprise, there were no pebbles on the floor. With this, they made their way out as fast as the older lady's legs would allow. When I interviewed them later, they were prepared to swear, even on a Bible, that every word was true!

A surprising number of people are of the opinion that many of the unexplained occurrences within the church may possibly have some connection with the Waldegrave family to whom there is a magnificent altar-tomb monument standing some 14 feet in height, with six Corinthian columns supporting a canopy. There are also two recumbent effigies in 16th-century dress and around the sides are kneeling figures, believed to be their three sons and three daughters.

The Waldegraves were a very influential family, Sir Edward having been knighted in 1553 at the Coronation of Queen Mary I in whose household – when she was Princess Mary – he had held a high position. Being a Papist, he had been imprisoned in the Tower of London by Edward VI but when Mary eventually came to the throne, he was of course released and all his powers restored. However, five years later when Queen Elizabeth came to the throne, he was once again sent to the Tower, where he remained until his death on 1st September 1561. His remains were eventually brought back to Borley for burial in a church that had by that time already adopted the revised prayer book of the reformed Church; this is what some people believe he cannot accept and the disturbances are his only way of showing his disapproval.

A sudden surge of interest in Borley church in the early 1990s unfortunately led to such an increase in vandalism that the authorities decided to keep the building locked except for when it was being used for services. This caused considerable inconvenience to several groups of psychic investigators who, for a long time, had been making regular visits at all hours of the day and night in order to study and record as much of the paranormal activity as possible.

One particular group from London had, over the years, gathered quite a collection of tape recordings covering a whole range of phenomena, including 'phantom' organ music, voices, clatterings, bangings, heavy door bolts apparently being drawn and so on. Now, although their activities were somewhat restricted to the outside of the church, this did not deter them.

Late one very warm August Saturday evening, four of them arrived and planned which of the areas they would patrol until such time as they felt that enough was enough for the night. For quite a while, nothing untoward happened – it was a quiet, bright moonlit night – until at about 3 o'clock in the morning the temperature suddenly dropped considerably. After having a break for a welcome cup of coffee, they decided to stay on for another half an hour and then pack up and go home.

After a further fruitless wait, they had just started gathering their gear together when one of the group had the impression that something or somebody was standing behind them. Quietly telling the others to stand still and keep quiet, she took two photographs of the door behind them. Nothing further being seen or heard, they finished packing and went back to London.

A week or so later, after having the film developed, the photographer was so astonished at what she saw on two of her 'shots' of the church door, that she immediately contacted me, sending one of the prints. After carefully examining it, I drove to Borley and, standing on the same spot as the young lady had done, I took a photograph of the same door. When that film was developed, it showed just what one would normally expect – the door as it is today.

A few days later when the vicar was shown the photographs, he couldn't understand what he was seeing because the young lady's photo clearly showed not only the door open with a light inside, but also three veiled figures, one of which looked like a bride holding what appeared to be a bouquet of flowers; also the shape of the doorway in the picture was different. He went on to add that so far as he was aware, the present door had not been opened for at least 80 years – perhaps longer – and, because the shape and size appeared to be different, he came to the conclusion that the whole thing was a fake! However, the group were very serious investigators and I personally had every reason to believe that the photograph was genuine

One can only speculate – was this perhaps a re-enactment of a long-ago wedding?

BRADFIELD

A Strange Case of Déjà Vu

Déjà vu, reincarnation, ESP (Extra Sensory Perception) – call it what you will, but by any name, the following true story, despite considerable research, almost defies explanation!
A few years ago in mid-summer, a 3½-year-old boy was being taken by his parents for his first trip to the seaside at Walton-on-the-Naze from their home in a village near Ipswich. His father was driving and his mother sat beside the boy in the back. Not wishing to get caught up in the busy traffic on the main roads, his father preferred to take a more leisurely and scenic route through the country lanes and villages.

As they were travelling along, the boy appeared to be getting somewhat agitated. His parents, thinking that he might be feeling travel-sick, stopped, but when they tried to get him out onto the verge, he became hysterical and refused to leave the car. His mother naturally tried to console him and asked what was the matter, but all the boy did was to mumble and, amid his tears, keep pointing towards a field.

His father, getting more impatient by the minute, shut the door, got back in and drove on. Gradually the boy calmed down and by the time they had reached their destination he was back to normal. The rest of the day, which was spent on the beach, passed pleasantly; the boy thoroughly enjoyed playing on the sand and having a paddle, but all good things must come to an end and they eventually made their way home by a totally different route with no further trouble.

It was some two years later and by then the boy was nearly six years old, when his parents decided to have another day at the seaside; this time the boy sat by himself in the back, his mother in the passenger seat beside his father. Deciding to take the same route as before, not even remembering the boy's upset, they set out on their journey.

All went well until they reached the spot where on the previous trip the lad had started his tantrums. Without any warning whatsoever, the boy started shouting and pointing across the field, just as he had done before. This time his father did not stop, but his mother turned around in her seat and asked what all the noise was about, to which the boy replied that he had worked on that field driving a tractor and that he was then known as 'Dopey Dan Dale'.

His mother told him not to be so silly. How could he possibly have worked there, he was not yet even six years of age, but the boy was adamant and even named the farm and the farmer. Bearing in mind they lived nearly twenty miles away and had only passed that field once before, there was no way he could have possibly known the name of the farm, let alone the farmer – which was something that even his parents did not know!

The whole episode worried his father to such an extent that he eventually started making enquiries. First of all, he found that the name of the farm was exactly as his son had said and although it now had a different occupier, a little research soon revealed that the boy had named the farmer who had actually farmed the land during the Second World War!

The next thing was to try to establish whether or not there had really been a Dan Dale with the nickname of 'Dopey'. This proved to be far more difficult; the majority of the residents of the village were now newcomers and after all, the boy's father was trying to locate one man (if indeed he ever existed) from over 50 years ago – almost 'mission impossible'! By pure chance, however, he was given the name and address of an elderly man who had been classed as unfit for military service and had been directed to work on that particular farm. A visit to the address revealed that the man had indeed worked there throughout the war years and although he recalled there being a young man whom they called 'Dopey', he could not remember his real name, although he did recall that he used to come from a nearby local institution that catered for 'backward or difficult' children of wealthy parents.

Armed with this information, it only took a little more research to verify the fact that a 'patient' by this name had in fact lived there at the time. After the war he had discharged himself and consequently they had no further record of him.

The intriguing question now is – what happened to Dan Dale? Is he still alive? Did he in fact die and had he been reincarnated, as the boy's experiences appear to suggest? Searches of local records have failed to reveal any marriage, death or burial details. Perhaps he left the area after the war. If he is still alive, he would now be in his late nineties. The boy – now a young man of course – refuses to discuss the matter. So far as he is concerned, he has his own life to live, the past is the past and so be it.

Just in case, by the remotest chance, anyone should recognise or remember anything whatsoever about a Dan Dale or the farm where he worked, which was at Bradfield, near Manningtree, or his last known address, which was Brunswick House, Mistley, sometime in the late 1940s or early 1950s, any information, however vague, regarding this gentleman would not only be greatly appreciated but of course treated with the utmost discretion.

BRADWELL-JUXTA-MARE

The Haunted Chapel

What is believed to be England's second oldest chapel – St Peter's-ad-Murum, better known as St Peter's-on-the-Wall, also as St Cedd's Chapel – is on the clifftop near to the village now known as Bradwell-on-Sea or, to give it its original name, Bradwell-juxta-Mare. For over 500 years, the chapel had the reputation for being haunted, probably not always by the same ghosts, although many reports of the alleged sightings bear a remarkable similarity.

Even its origins have a ring of the unusual about them. It is widely believed that in or about AD 654, St Cedd, a disciple of St Dunstan, left the beautiful abbey of Lindisfarne on Holy Island, just off the Northumberland coast, and landed on the Essex coast near to the then abandoned Roman fort of Othona and 'to the glory of God' collected stones from the ruins and built a small chapel.

Over the centuries and with the passing of time, although most of the original chapel has been destroyed by the combined efforts of the elements and vandals, what remains seems to have been patched up and the building put to good use – albeit as a barn, a cowshed, a coastguard's lookout post and during the Victorian period even as storage for the local smugglers. After the Second World War it was often used by groups of wildfowlers who made it their overnight base and, as one can well imagine, it was not long before tales about ghostly sightings started to circulate.

There have been many reports of what appears to be a spectral horse, appearing to come from the old Roman settlement on Mersea Island and galloping at full speed towards the site of the fort of Othona, thus giving credence to the legend of a phantom Roman cavalryman riding to warn the garrison of impending danger. Various people have also claimed to have witnessed a ghostly Roman centurion still carrying out his watch-keeping during the night in the vicinity of the old Roman fort!

In 1963, several reports were printed in the local newspapers about the strange events that were said to have occurred at an isolated house that had originally been built as a farm worker's cottage, just a short distance from the chapel. The cottage which had fallen into disrepair had recently been renovated and was now used as a holiday home.

A gentleman said that while staying in it, he had been awakened by the growling of his dog and saw in the bright moonlight a man apparently staring intently at him through the window. He appeared to have a particularly large nose and the expression on his face suggested extreme sadness; he was dressed in what looked like a seaman's jacket with a double row of brass buttons.

It was only as the gentleman started to get out of bed that the 'visitor' outside the cottage ostensibly *floated* through the window and, although standing only about a yard away, completely ignored him, just as if he didn't exist! Suddenly and only when he turned and seemed to be having a good look around the room, it became apparent that he only appeared to be solid from the waist upwards, whereas his lower extremities were just a misty blur!

While all this was happening, the dog, having hidden under the bed with just an occasional whimper, suddenly plucked up sufficient courage to let out a growl, whereupon the intruder, having obviously heard or sensed the dog, half turned and 'floated' back the same way as he had entered.

Since then, there have been several similar reports of people having unexplained experiences while staying in that particular cottage but unfortunately, as so often happens, they have kept their identity quiet for fear of ridicule.

However, one gentleman who did recount his experience said that on a particularly hot stifling mid-July night while sleeping in the back room, he was awakened by an intense coldness. Sitting up in bed, he was struck a blow on the jaw by what he was convinced was a man's fist, despite the fact that there was no sign of an assailant! Recovering from the shock, he pulled himself together sufficiently to try to think about what to do, not only because the window and door were still shut and there was no other means of exit from the room, but because who or whatever had hit him must still be in there. Cautiously switching on the light and looking round, it was obvious that he was quite alone – the door was still locked, as was the window; the only proof he had of the incident was a very swollen, aching jaw!

Many other people have tried to explain how uncomfortable they have felt while sleeping in those bedrooms. One, a bird-watcher who stayed overnight, recalled that he was awakened by the sound of galloping hoof-beats that were so loud that he thought they were going to crash into the cottage. Jumping out of bed and running to the window, there was no sign of any horses, despite the fact that he could still hear the sound fading into the distance.

In June 1967 a man, having pitched his tent near the chapel and smoking his last cigarette of the day while admiring the brilliant array of stars overhead, also heard hoof-beats. His first thoughts were that it was an idiotic time to be out horse riding and at speed as well but although the sound appeared to go past him and despite the bright moonlight, he saw nothing of either the horse or rider.

On numerous occasions, a mysterious light appears to shine from the old chapel windows even though there is no power supply and, when it is searched for possible intruders, there is nobody to be seen or anything else to account for the light.

Usually the atmosphere within the chapel is very friendly, but some who have spent the night there claim to have felt a malevolent presence and, in some cases, actually seen dim, indistinct shadowy figures against the walls.

BRENTWOOD

Spirits at the White Hart

The White Hart inn at Brentwood, with its nine busy bars, four restaurants and a constant flow of traffic through the courtyard, is not the easiest of places to track down spirits – apart from, of course, the inviting contents of the optics. However, several recent managers and members of staff tell some very strange stories that could well have some foundation in view of the building's great age which, according to Nikolaus Pevsner, is pre-1500. In fact, Richard II, whose coat of arms included a white hart, is believed to have stayed there on 19th November 1392 and the inn acquired its name after his visit.

At one time, horse-drawn stage and mail coaches travelling between London and Norwich and the East Coast used it and its most striking feature is still the galleried yard, which, until recent years, was used for the performance of Shakespeare's plays. Despite now being enclosed, the basic structure of the gallery is probably little changed from the days when coaches drove under the arch to change horses.

Although so-called progress has incorporated the White Hart into a chain of ye-olde-worlde-style restaurants, many of the original beams, including the timbers from old ships, have been retained. The oldest part, which is now the Steak Bar, used to be a kitchen with a linen cupboard. A lady who claimed to be psychic has said that this cupboard area was the scene of something dreadful – rape or murder, at the very least – while others connect it with a servant girl whose spirit is said to haunt the place.

One manager had the impression that at least one of the ghosts was male and was of the opinion that, considering the inn's history of one-night stops (stagecoaches), drunken brawls and general violence, which today we tend to regard with some degree of tolerance in the mellow glow of 'romance', the White Hart could easily be the location of several male or female spectres.

One particularly playful spirit appears to spend a lot of its earth-bound time moving the tables around overnight and, just to keep the waiting staff on their toes, likes to rattle the cutlery in the drawer even while the staff are standing nearby.

A door some 8 ft above the floor in the Steak Bar, and which is actually the access to a hot water tank, is often found wide open, despite being locked and needing a ladder to reach it. Wine bottles have been seen to tumble from their racks, bounce and land the right way up and unbelievably, remain unbroken!

Another part of the building said to be haunted is the ballroom. A former manageress told me that on numerous occasions neither she nor her staff were able to cross its floor because it was just as if an invisible barrier stopped them from going in either direction; although on the odd occasion this would only last a few seconds, at others it could be up to twenty minutes. Unnerving as it was, she said the worst part was not knowing when it was there or when it had gone, because there was no warning either way: 'One minute we could cross the floor normally, the next it was like walking into a plate glass window.' A waitress, while crossing the floor and having been tapped on her shoulder, looked round and found nobody close enough to have done it!

Footsteps heard ascending the stairs, when there was nobody there or at least not visibly so, is a phenomenon that has occurred many times near the Steak Bar and has been heard by both staff and customers alike.

Even the management's living quarters are not immune. One manager recalled how he was woken up in the middle of the night to find his room unusually cold and with an uncanny atmosphere, but when he switched on the light, everything appeared to be normal.

Several generations of management and staff alike have testified over the years to the inexplicable. Ghosts are, of course, no respecters of age, sex or even sites. How else can anybody explain haunted inns, pubs, council houses or even London Underground stations? It looks as if most occurrences and tragedies have occurred in what are now the most benign, prosaic places.

CHELMSFORD

Moral: Don't Upset Your Mother-in-Law!

A particularly bizarre event hit the headlines in the national newspapers during 1996, when a retired Essex policeman turned exorcist and banished a poltergeist from his neighbour's home in Chelmsford.

It all started on the night of 5th November, bonfire night, when his neighbour's family had been out enjoying the local display of pyrotechnics. On their return, they opened the front door to be greeted not only by water pouring through the lounge ceiling, but to find the furniture splattered with what appeared to be runny eggs, milk, tea leaves and also what, to say the least, appeared to be chocolate mousse!

This was all far too much for them to cope with at this time of night, so they went to sleep at the house of relatives living nearby. Returning the following morning and cautiously opening the door, they found the place an absolute shambles – smashed crockery was everywhere, pictures ripped from the walls, furniture upturned, in fact the whole place was somewhat reminiscent of being hit by a wartime bomb.

Despite the fact that water was still dripping from the ceiling, when they looked upstairs the floor was completely dry. Thinking that a pipe must have burst between the floor and the ceiling, they immediately sent for a plumber, who – surprisingly – quickly arrived and, having agreed with their assessment, rolled back the bedroom carpet and took up a couple of floorboards. He was, however, unable to discover the source of the still running water, despite the fact that every possible stopcock had been turned off.

In case he had missed one somewhere, he went through the house again, opening and examining every cupboard, but when he came to the last one he was pelted with crockery of all kinds, which literally flew across the room, smashing against the wall and anything else in its path.

At this point, the householders decided that a new approach to the situation was needed and called in their local vicar. He, unfortunately, was forced to admit that he had never come across a situation such as this before and would have to seek help from a more senior priest, and that would take time! However, their neighbour, a retired policeman, having obviously noticed all the activity next door, asked if everything was all right and was there anything he could do to help? When told of the situation, he said that he had some knowledge of spiritualism and would try to see what he could do.

After saying a short prayer, he went into a trance and was apparently soon able to contact the spirit who was causing all the trouble. It turned out to be the husband's late mother-in-law who had passed away some three years earlier. She told him that she could not accept the fact that whenever she had tried to contact the family, they just ignored her. Eventually she became so frustrated that she found the power to create sufficient havoc until they would acknowledge her!

After a lengthy session, he managed to calm her down and explained that she had passed over and her family were quite unaware that she had been trying to communicate with them. If she would now leave them in peace, he would pass on her message. Apparently she accepted his explanation and peace reigned once again.

The Missing Architect

In the late 1970s a very strange and bizarre story unfolded in Chelmsford – a tragic event that, without doubt, led to the haunting of a very fine detached house, which for obvious reasons must remain unidentified.

A highly successful architect who lived in Chelmsford had his office in London's West End where, over the years, he had built a reputation for his designs, not only in this country, but also in France where his services were in great demand. Being very much a 'hands on' man, he liked to spend as much time as possible near to where the buildings he had designed were being built and to facilitate this he had a replica of his Chelmsford home built in France.

When in England, he spent much of his spare time practising his favourite hobby – DIY – in fact, he was almost a fanatic, adding extra cupboards, filling in odd corners and even utilising any available piece of roof space.

Arriving home unexpectedly from France, he was horrified to discover his wife in bed with another man, the shock of which must have mentally unbalanced him. Going to a cupboard, he took out his double-barrelled, 12-bore shotgun and, having loaded it, quietly climbed the stairs and, pushing open the bedroom door, took aim and squeezed the trigger twice.

Although obviously totally insane, he nevertheless went back to the kitchen, stripped the gun and, having thoroughly cleaned and oiled it, returned it to the cupboard. He then apparently went into his yard and getting a quantity of breeze-blocks, he took them upstairs into a room where he had already started to build a wall between a chimneybreast and another wall. Mixing up some mortar, he carried on building.

It would appear that he then got a chair and a length of cord and continued to build the wall from the inside without leaving an exit. Having finally sealed himself in, he obviously looped the cord over a ceiling joist and secured the end. He then stood upon the chair and, having put the other end of the cord round his neck in the form of a noose, he either jumped from the chair or kicked it away.

It was not until some weeks later that the bodies of the wife and her lover were discovered and the police, having started a murder hunt and thinking that the architect was still in France, made every effort to locate and inform him of the tragedy.

At this stage, in the belief that he was still involved with his work in France, he was not considered a suspect until some weeks later when the French police advised that he had not been seen at either his house or on the building sites for some weeks. Their investigations led them to believe that he had returned to England. With this information, the local police then placed him at the top of the list of suspects and a full-scale search for him started.

A couple more weeks passed and, with still no sign of him and the police getting desperate for a lead, a detective, believing in the theory that if you get stuck, return to basics, revisited the house, hoping to find any clue that might have been missed in the earlier searches. He was in an upstairs room when he noticed a foul smell apparently coming from behind an unplastered wall and, getting a heavy hammer, he soon knocked a hole in the block-work to see inside the recess, where he was horrified to discover the now putrefied remains of the missing architect.

Although it now did not take the police very long to piece together the whole sorry story, *our* story does not end there. In due course, the house was sold and a family moved in. All went well for some months until late one afternoon a unearthly scream was heard coming from a bedroom, followed by what sounded like a woman's voice screaming 'No, no,' after which all went quiet.

A few hours later, the distinct sound of a timber beam creaking as if under a sudden strain was followed by the twang as of a rope suddenly tightening, after which a horrible thud came from the room where the demented architect ended his life.

Although similar sounds have since been heard on numerous occasions, they have been very irregular.

CLACTON-ON-SEA

The Mystery of the Butcher's Shop

When in the early 1970s a run-down farm on the outskirts of Clacton-on-Sea was sold for building purposes, it was not long before, amongst the quickly-erected bungalows and houses, a parade of shops was built to serve the needs of newly-arrived residents in what was to become Blue House Avenue.

For various reasons, these shops frequently changed hands. Different trades, grocers, newsagents, ladies' hairdressers, greengrocers and butchers, all came and went. It was not necessarily lack of trade that caused the changes in ownership; illness, death, domestic problems, partnerships breaking up and so on all took their toll. Eventually four adjoining shops became empty and remained so for nearly a year.

At length, in the late 1980s, a young couple who already had a general shop elsewhere in the area took over the lease of all four shops and turned them into a moderately successful mini-market. However, a spate of shoplifting led them to install a video camera security system throughout the shop with a control point in the manager's office.

It was while watching the monitor of the camera covering a large freezer unit that the manager saw a man's severed head on the middle shelf and that was not his only shock. On the top shelf of the same unit was the body of a woman with long fair hair hanging down between the wire shelves, and her hands and feet appeared to be tied with a rope that criss-crossed her chest.

More than a little shaken, the manager adjusted the control to get a closer view and as the camera traversed the adjoining freezer, much to his horror, on the middle shelf was yet another man's severed head!

This was far too much for him. He frantically phoned the owners and begged for someone to come over as quickly as possible, stressing that it was *very* urgent. When the lady arrived and went into the office to find the manager pointing to the screen, with the camera picking up not only on the two heads but also the woman's body, she too was badly shaken.

Pulling themselves together, they went into the shop and made their way towards the freezer section covered by the camera, where to their utter surprise there was no sign of men's heads or a woman's body; the shelves were stacked with frozen food as normal with nothing out of place. Mystified, they returned to the office and again looked at the screen on which both the heads and the body were still there for all to see! Switching off the system, they took the cassette out and locked it in the safe.

Subsequent research revealed that the freezer was positioned on what had once been part of a butcher's shop that had suddenly closed in mysterious circumstances. Late one night the butcher had apparently shot himself in the shop, despite the fact that the business appeared to have been doing well. He had always appeared to get along very well with his customers, although he was occasionally a little uncouth and given to quietly swearing – usually to himself – for no apparent reason.

It was not long before rumours started to circulate that perhaps the butcher had discovered that his wife might have been having an affair with two men. This could have been a situation with which he was unable to cope and his mind became so deranged that he took his own life. Local people and also some of his customers began to recollect that immediately prior to and since the butcher's death, they had seen neither his wife nor her two alleged lovers. Was it possible that the butcher, having found out about his wife's possible infidelity, had taken matters into his own hands? After all, who would be better placed to dispose of bodies than a butcher?

One can only conjecture whether or not the scene the manager and shop owner both saw on the video screen was a re-enactment of a situation and whether the woman's body was that of his wife and the two heads those of her lovers.

As may well be expected, one of the Sunday national newspapers really went to town on the case but, despite all their efforts, the identity of neither man was ever traced nor what happened to the butcher's wife!

Oh, the video tape in the safe. When the police eventually examined it, it was found to be completely blank.

The Sequel

Some months later and after I became involved in the above story, there were reports that not only were vague shadows seen at the freezer end of the shop but also what appeared to be a gruff voice was heard, apparently swearing. This was despite the fact that the staff, having thoroughly searched the place, found nothing to account for either the shadows or the swearing, which incidentally always occurred in the evening just before closing time – 11 pm.

Later still, I visited the premises just before closing time with a psychic medium. He was not a local man and knew nothing of the story. Having parked his car some fifty yards away and while walking across the forecourt, he stopped dead in his tracks and started to shake. Stepping backwards about a yard or so he returned to normal, but when slowly moving forward, he again began to shake uncontrollably until taking two paces further forward he again returned to normal. He explained that he had picked up a very strong ley line that apparently ran diagonally under the shop and that it was about 3 ft feet wide.

While wandering around the shop, he again picked up the ley line and followed it from where it entered, passing through a store room which was once part of the old butcher's shop, under the freezer section where the two units stood, across the shop and out to the rear wall near the manager's office.

Carefully avoiding the ley line, he went behind the freezer units and stopped. He then signalled an area where he felt that something terrible had happened in the fairly recent past – the area was where the butcher would normally have worked. One can only conjecture whether the medium was picking up vibrations of murders or perhaps the death of the butcher.

I must emphasise that the medium knew nothing of the history of the shop or even where I was taking him; as far as he was concerned, he was only assisting in an investigation.

A Sequel to a Sequel!

When later I was in conversation with the shop owners, the husband said that whenever he used to go to the shop to tidy up, cash up and generally deal with any problems the staff may have had during the day, he never felt comfortable being there alone – he often had the impression that he was *not* alone. He did not consider himself a nervous type, but ...

He recalled the evening when a customer had rushed over and said that a man carrying a shotgun and looking like the butcher who had committed suicide had just walked into the warehouse at the end of the shop, which used to be the former butcher's shop. They both went there quickly but found no sign of anyone. It later turned out that other people had seen what could only have been the same apparition, although sometimes without a gun. All agreed on one thing – it was the manifestation of the dead butcher!

Just before the new owners had reopened the shop, a number of alterations were made and the windows were whitewashed over. Within a few days, faces began to appear in the whitewash and although nobody admitted doing them, they were artistic *and* recognisable. On one photograph that was taken from outside the shop, one of the faces was identified as being that of one of the severed heads later seen on the shelf in the freezer unit!

Later, when the photo was turned upside down, another face could clearly be seen and was identified by the couple who lived in the flat over the shop as that of the apparition they had both seen coming out of their wardrobe (of which, more below). This led to considerable speculation as to why the face should appear upside down – had it been the face of a man hung from a butcher's hook?

The lady owner recalled the occasion when she had been in the office with the manager and the subject of the various unexplained occurrences was brought up; she had just said that despite what had apparently occurred in the shop, she found it hard to accept that there was no logical explanation for most of it when suddenly two penny coins dropped onto the desk in front of them which were stuck together!

Then there was the time when an ice cream salesman left his order book and the bill on the desk while he went out to his van to make up the shop's order. When he returned, the book and bill were missing and, thinking that someone was playing about, he got annoyed, despite the fact that no one had touched them. The owner and manager searched everywhere, even to the extent of emptying dustbins and sifting through the contents, but with no success. However, later that evening, after the shop was closed and while they were cashing up, in the centre of the desk was not only the order book but also the missing bill!

During November 1992 I was asked to visit the flat over the shop to investigate the various phenomena that Mark and Jenny, together with Jenny's two sons, aged 8 and 6 years, claimed were making their lives, to use their own words, 'a living hell'. They had taken on the lease of the flat some nine months earlier, the previous tenant – an elderly gentleman – had left rather hurriedly, without giving any explanation whatsoever, after staying there for only three weeks. Mark and Jenny had moved in two weeks later.

Almost immediately, they experienced what they described as 'psychic disturbances'. Jenny, in particular, sensed that there was something that was not human in the flat and said that she had seen 'things' in the rooms, although these sightings stopped for a while after a friend carried out a form of exorcism. However, they soon began to appear again and she saw what she described as a 'black and white striped cloak' near the stairs, also shapes that seemed to play 'hide and seek' when she entered a room and would appear to peek around armchairs and doors.

She said that she never saw anything long enough to say exactly what it was, but Mark stated that on one occasion he noticed a male shape that also wanted to play games like peeping around doors, then dashing away to briefly reappear elsewhere. This had been about a month before our meeting.

Mark also said that although he often sensed 'things' in their lounge, bedroom and on the stairs, somehow he did not think they were the same entities because the 'feeling' was so different! He went on to explain that it was like a shuddering when the entity was close to him – he would come over hot and sweaty on the inside and cold on the outside, causing him to shake and at times see various colours, purple, green, red and a misty grey, which would seem to flash about the room.

In addition, he recalled the occasion when he saw what appeared to be a man standing between their bedroom and that of their children. The figure was wearing a black cloak, but appeared to be faceless. About two months earlier (September 1992) he had seen a similar figure in the flat, wearing what appeared to be a dark robe and a flat hat with a wide brim, similar to those worn by Quakers.

In their bedroom was a wardrobe-cum-dressing table, from which figures used to emerge. A medium who visited the flat told them they should get rid of the wardrobe. A few nights later, their sleep was disturbed by a violent vibrating emanating from the wardrobe which, the following morning, they moved into the lounge. Even this did not stop the vibrations; in fact, they became worse – so bad indeed that the occupants of the next door flat complained that ornaments were being shaken from the shelf on *their* side of the wall!

The question arose as to the possible history of the wardrobe: apparently, it was bought in a saleroom by Jenny's parents as a present and delivered to the flat the day before Jenny and Mark moved in. After the neighbours' complaint, they decided to put it into a forthcoming auction, but before they did, they had a hair-raising experience. Mark was resting on the settee in the lounge, when Jenny saw a big black figure coming from the wardrobe. Petrified and clutching Mark's foot, she gave it a hard shake to make sure that he was awake enough to see the apparition.

As it passed behind Jenny, Mark jumped up and took a swipe at it, but the strange thing was, as he admitted afterwards, although he hit out at it, he never actually saw the figure. He just heard a movement and saw a band of coloured lights similar to those he had seen on the stairs. The band seemed to be about 18 ins to 2 ft wide but when he struck out, it turned and wrapped itself around his legs, winding its way up to his waist, up his back and then disappeared across the room. This exhibition was followed by a number of faces appearing all around the room and Jenny saw a grinning face in the window. Whilst this was all happening, their pet budgie flew about its cage, making the most awful noise.

They agreed that although all this sounded absolutely stupid, almost impossible, it really did happen. Neither of them took drugs or smoked and only had an occasional drink – there was no obvious explanation.

They related that on earlier occasions, long after the shop below had closed for the night, they would clearly hear a woman's footsteps walking about the premises; it was quite a distinctive walk, not unlike that of the shop owner. When they mentioned this to her, she replied that she, too, often woke up during the night thinking that she had actually been in the shop. She imagined she had been dreaming, but now wondered if she had 'astral travelled' or had had an out-of-body experience.

Mark also told me of the occasion when they were visited by some friends with their 8-year-old daughter; the child ran into the lounge, saying that she had just seen a strange lady walk into a bedroom. When they looked, there was nobody there! Then there was the occasion that

Jenny was out shopping and Mark was alone in the kitchen when he saw a shadow in the hallway. This was not the first time he had spotted a similar shadow in the same area, but on this occasion, thinking that Jenny had returned, he called out, but there was no answer. Through the open bedroom door he saw somebody who – because of the long hair and figure – he thought was Jenny, but as the figure moved he realised that it was the shadow of a man with long hair who was apparently walking through the open bedroom door and disappearing.

With the tension building and fearing that the boys would become seriously affected, Mark and Jenny started looking for another flat or house to rent.

The Human Arm

Perhaps the following story may sound incredible, but this Clacton man, who for obvious reasons asked for neither his name nor address to be revealed, swears that every word is the absolute truth. I was equally sceptical and checked with the local police who, although they confirmed that according to their records the gentleman in question had in fact deposited the remains of a human arm with them on the date stated, would reveal no further details because their enquiries were still continuing. It must be added that they subjected me to a lengthy investigation before even these meagre details were confirmed.

However, this is the account as given by the gentleman concerned. One evening in 1986, he took his dog for its customary evening run along the beach between Clacton and Jaywick and, as often happened, the dog ran off – possibly chasing rabbits over the golf course – only to make its own way home some hours later.

On this particular occasion, it was nearly midnight before there was the usual scratching on the front door, signalling that the dog wanted to be let in. When the man opened the door, he was not surprised at first to see that the dog had something in its mouth – it often brought home a rabbit. This time, though, what the dog was holding was a human forearm, no less, which looked as if it had been wrenched away at the elbow! The fact that there was still flesh and skin on it suggested that it had not long been detached from the rest of the arm; also strips of seaweed made it obvious that it had been in the sea.

Bearing in mind that it was now the early hours of the morning, the dog's owner decided that it was far too late to do anything about it that night. He therefore carefully wrapped the arm in a plastic bag and put it in his freezer with the intention of taking it to the police station as soon as possible.

He hadn't been in bed very long; in fact, it felt as if he had only just dropped off to sleep, when both he and his wife were awakened by the sound of a strange rapping, followed by an unaccountable series of quite loud moans and groans. He got out of bed to investigate but the noises ceased as soon as he started to go down the stairs. No sooner had he gone back to bed, though, than they started all over again.

Later that morning he took the arm to the police and after a very lengthy session trying to convince them of the facts, he returned home. That night the rapping, moans and groans returned – even louder than before. It seemed as if his dog had not only brought home an arm, but also the ghost of its owner! This situation continued for some weeks - night after night their sleep was disturbed – until it suddenly stopped for a couple of months.

Because their lives had been so disrupted, it was decided that his wife and two children should go and stay for a while with relatives and, in the meantime, the husband would install a long-promised central heating system. However, the very first night the family were away, to quote his own words, 'all hell was let loose'. The rappings, banging, moans and groans were much louder than ever before. Although he had grown accustomed to the disturbance, he had a niggling feeling that perhaps burglars, thinking that all members of the family were away, had broken in. He jumped out of bed, grabbed a length of timber and ran though the house, shouting at the top of his voice that he would kill them if he found them, but nobody was there. It was only when he reached the bottom of the stairs that he realised that the noises had stopped.

When he eventually calmed down and had made himself a cup of tea to steady his shattered nerves, he decided to come to terms with the situation. Standing in the kitchen, looking towards the deep-freezer, he said, 'All right, I haven't got your arm, you do not belong here, so please leave me and my family in peace!' With that he switched off the light and went to bed.

Over the next few nights, although the noises still persisted, they became less intense with each succeeding night until they finally ceased altogether.

The Tragic Story of June Lacey

The following true story has been recorded and reproduced with the full permission of the families concerned and their co-operation was greatly appreciated. To quote the old adage, 'truth is stranger than fiction' and this series of events is no exception, as the reader will surely appreciate.

It all started in the summer of 1942 in wartime Clacton-on-Sea when the threat of invasion was never very far away. Clacton, like many other East Coast towns, was bristling with troops. Its usually sandy beaches were covered with masses of steel tube scaffolding and coil after coil of barbed wire; and beneath those golden sands many land mines were just waiting for the enemy to place an unwary boot.

In 1940 most of the civilian population, especially the children, had been evacuated; in fact, there was hardly a child anywhere in the area. However, despite the Government's advice and wishes, and notwithstanding the possibility of invasion, by 1942 a few people had for various reasons returned. It was into these dangerous conditions that two families, the Irishes and the Chuggs, came back with their respective daughters, June Lacey (Mrs Irish's daughter by a previous marriage) and Christine Chugg, both aged about 14 years.

The summer of 1942 was one of the hottest on record and the troops, with very little to do other than watch and wait for the enemy, found themselves with time on their hands. Their officers, realising only too well they would have to do something to relieve the tension, allowed a small area of beach near the pier to be cleared of mines, and the troops, in small numbers, were permitted to go swimming, which of course was greatly appreciated by all.

June and Christine, who had got to know one another, soon made friends, together with a few other children, with the soldiers, who persuaded those in charge to allow the youngsters to play on the beach and have a swim. All went well for some time, until one fateful day when the two girls went down to the beach as usual and chatted with some of the troops before going for a swim. Coming out of the water, they lay upon the beach for a while before playing around with a beach ball and thoroughly enjoying themselves. After some time had passed, June decided to go by herself for another swim and because the tide was well on its way out, she had to walk almost beyond the end of the pier before the water was deep enough.

When conditions are like that, there are very dangerous undercurrents. Sadly nobody on shore realised the danger until it was far too late – June was caught and, not being a strong enough swimmer, was sucked under and carried away before anyone could reach her.

It was some five days later before her body was washed up on the beach opposite the Eastcliff Hotel at Holland-on-Sea, some two miles away from where she had disappeared.

Both Mrs Irish and Mrs Chugg, the two mothers, regularly attended a local Spiritualist church; in fact, Mrs Irish was a highly respected medium. One Sunday evening, some five years later, they were both attending a service given by a visiting medium who, knowing nothing whatsoever of the tragedy, told Mrs Irish that her daughter would be attending the wedding of – when she got married – her friend's daughter, although this would probably be some time in the future.

Mrs Irish, being a very experienced medium, did not reject this message out of hand, although she later expressed doubts about how June could possibly be at Christine's wedding, having died all those years ago.

A further two years passed and the medium's message was nearly forgotten, until another visiting medium gave Mrs Irish an almost identical message. This was far too much of a coincidence and the communications were talked over between the two families many times, bearing in mind that there was no sign of Christine getting married.

When, in 1954, Christine did accept a proposal of marriage, it was not long before the prediction was remembered and everyone speculated as to what might happen and in what form.

The day of the wedding, a fine, sunny Saturday, came and, with the ceremony due to take place at the Baptist church in Pier Avenue, a crowd was waiting for the bride to arrive. When at last the car with Christine, her bridesmaids and mother drew up at the kerbside, the driver (the late Mr C.F. Barnes) jumped out and came round to open the door.

Just as the smiling Christine stepped out, she appeared to stumble and was only stopped from falling by the timely action of Mr Barnes. When she recovered her composure, the camera clicked and she, half laughing, carried on as if nothing had happened. The ceremony went ahead without further incident and a very happy bride and groom emerged from the church to pose for more photographs.

While the reception was taking place, the photographer, Mr McGowan of Meacock & McGowan, went back to his shop in High Street where he developed the films and, on returning to the reception with the prints, he pinned them on a board for all to see.

When the guests saw the photos, they stood back in astonishment. On the first photo – that of Christine leaving the car – there, clearly on the front of her wedding dress was an imprint of a girl's face with a rubber bathing cap and the face was that of June Lacey, the friend who had so tragically drowned some twelve years earlier!

Mr McGowan, somewhat bewildered, hastily went back to his shop and, having closely examined the negatives, made duplicate prints, but with exactly the same result.

A week later, a guest having had *his* film developed found that sure enough, there was the same face, just as clear as before. Two cameras could not possibly have been faulty.

However, this was not the only surprise the photographs revealed. On closer examination, another smaller face, which was quickly identified as June Lacey's grandmother who had died a year or two after the drowning, was visible on the bride's right arm. She had been closely attached to June and had taken her death very badly. Yet another strange thing was the appearance of June's initials on one of the 'horseshoes' on the wedding dress; also the bride's right hand was not her hand at all, she having short squat fingers, whereas the hand on the photograph had long, thin fingers. Could these have also been those of the grandmother?

As if all this was not enough, further information has since come to light. When, in 1945, Mrs Chugg was staying the night with her friend Mrs Irish and sleeping in the middle bedroom, which had been June's, she had a restless night. Whether or not it was because she was in a strange bed, she just could not sleep. However, sometime between one and two o'clock in the morning, she became aware of what appeared to be a woman – dressed in a skirt and blouse with a shawl over her shoulder – *gliding* from the closed door towards the wardrobe. Slowly the wardrobe door swung open, revealing a rail full of girl's clothes, through which the woman appeared to rummage as if searching for a particular item.

Mrs Chugg could hardly believe her eyes. In fact, she thought she was having a nightmare, until she realised the woman, without a shadow of doubt, was June's grandmother. Although they had only met very briefly before she had died, just over a year earlier, here she – or at least her apparition – was, back in her dead granddaughter's bedroom, looking as real as ever.

Clearing her throat, Mrs Chugg quietly said, 'Hello, what are you looking for?' at which the figure turned and faded away.

Sleep for the rest of the night was out of the question, she just lay waiting for the dawn, during which time the ghostly figure returned twice more, each time searching the wardrobe apparently without success, before gliding back to the door and passing through it as if it did not exist!

The Decorator's Nightmare

Despite an acute shortage of rented accommodation in the 1970s, a house in Wellesley Road, Clacton-on-Sea, stood empty for many months. Tenants came and went, none staying more than a few weeks at the most and even then leaving in a hurry, some without even giving prior notice. Eventually the owner decided to sell the property but, despite instructing several estate agents, none managed to attract a buyer, even after several months of trying. Finally it was put up for auction and sold to a buyer from London who wasted no time in asking a local man to redecorate the house throughout.

As soon as he arrived, the decorator had the strange and uncomfortable impression that he was being watched. While working upstairs, he thought he heard voices downstairs but, when he went to investigate, he found nothing to account for what he was certain he had heard. Coming to the conclusion that it must have been the voices of passers-by echoing through the empty rooms, he returned to his work. As the day wore on, however, he became more certain that the voices were definitely coming from inside the house – mainly in the front room but at other times in the kitchen.

By the end of the day, he had become so nervous that he went home early. The next morning didn't start much better either. On opening the front door, much to his surprise and annoyance, all the equipment he had left neatly stacked in a back room was in a heap in the hallway. His first thoughts were that it was the work of vandals but, after looking around, he found no sign of a forced entry and, as far as he was aware, he was the only key holder.

Baffled, he tidied up and carried on where he had left off the day before. The rest of the day passed without further incident, as did the rest of the week, but he still had an uneasy feeling about the house.

The following Monday, a carpenter came to install some new cupboards and carry out minor repairs downstairs but, every now and then, thinking that the decorator had called him, he would either shout out or go up the stairs to ask what he wanted. He quickly finished his work and left in a hurry.

During the next few days many unaccountable things occurred: pots of paint left in one room would be found in another room; scaffold boards and trestles set up for doing ceilings upstairs would overnight end up downstairs; rolls of wallpaper were unrolled and draped over the banister; and packets of wallpaper paste were opened up and emptied onto the floor in almost perfect circles.

The end of the job couldn't come quickly enough for the poor decorator, bearing in mind everything that had occurred in those three weeks – despite the fact that in all this time neither he nor the carpenter actually saw anything move or even heard a sound of movement other than the voices!

Having finished all his work late in the afternoon on the day before the new owners were due to move in, he left the final tidying up and removal of his tools and equipment for the next morning when he would have a last-minute look round to make sure everything was in order.

On arriving with his car and trailer the next morning, he went to open the front door but, no matter how hard he tried, there was no way that it would open. Thinking that perhaps the paint had stuck, he put his shoulder to the door but with no effect. Now desperate, he went round to the back of the house and climbed over the fence to check the back door and ground floor windows, only to find that they were all secure. Returning to the front of the house, he could not believe his eyes – the door was wide open, his gear all neatly stacked in the hall. Making his way from room to room, he found they had all been swept out, windows cleaned without even a smear and every paint splash removed – the place was immaculate.

Saying a silent *thank you* to whoever had done all this overnight, he loaded his trailer and, as arranged, leaving the key on the mantelpiece, he made for the front door. Just as he was about to shut it, a strong fragrance of perfume wafted past him and the door gently closed of its own accord!

COLCHESTER

A Strange Occurrence in a Shop

One evening early in the 1990s something very unusual happened in a flat over a shop in Bergholt Road on the outskirts of Colchester. A shopkeeper, while attending a meeting in the town, had left his wife alone in the flat and it was while she was sitting in the lounge, watching television, that she thought she heard footsteps in the adjoining bedroom.

The two bedroom flat had only one entrance – through the shop and up the stairs into the lounge – therefore in order to get into the bedroom, anyone would have had to go through the lounge, which the lady had not left all evening. Realising this, she immediately thought that it must be either a burglar or a ghost and, as she was quite unaware of any history of the flat being haunted, she feared the worst!

Taking no chances, she picked up a heavy torch and edged her way into the bedroom from where the footsteps appeared to have come. Finding no sign of anybody or anything that could have accounted for the noise, she took the precaution of removing the key from the inside of the door and locking it on the lounge side. She then searched the smaller bedroom and, finding nothing there either, she also locked that door, after which, now feeling more secure and wondering whether perhaps her imagination was running riot, she returned to continue watching television.

Later that evening, when she again heard footsteps that appeared to come from the larger bedroom, she switched off the TV and, grabbing the torch, stood and waited, knowing full well that whoever was in that bedroom would have to smash the door down to get out. However, although she waited and waited, nothing further happened.

Being a very self sufficient lady, she sat down and was just about to switch the television back on, when there was a loud whooshing noise, the bedroom door shook and rattled and an icy wind appeared to sweep through the lounge, down the stairs into the shop, followed by an almighty crash from the doors at the rear of the shop!

Again, not only furious but intrigued, she went down the stairs and into the shop, where fortunately the lights at the back had been left on in readiness for her husband's return. She was able to see that the double doors at the rear, which opened outwards and had not only been locked but also barred, had been forced open and were literally hanging off their hinges, despite the fact that the lock and bar were still intact.

She then went further into the yard, and the security light activated, which it had not done earlier! She searched the yard but found no sign of anyone or anything to account for the damage to the door or the noise. The yard was not only completely enclosed by a high concrete block wall but had heavy wooden doors, which were over 6 ft in height and with spikes on the top.

Going back into the shop, she could see no sign of anything having been touched or moved in any way; even papers on the counter were undisturbed despite the obvious strength of the 'wind' that had passed down the stairs. It soon became apparent that the icy blast had only been in a very narrow strip and had wound its way across the lounge, down the stairs, through the shop until it came against the rear doors, the first solid object it had encountered, and then, with unbelievable force, burst them open!

Despite intensive research, nothing has yet been found to account for this sudden outburst, apart from perhaps one event – possibly completely unrelated – three days earlier, the lady's mother had died.

The Haunted Police Station

When in the late 1980s I was told of 'unexplained happenings' in Colchester's police station which had been built on a site previously occupied by a row of cottages and a derelict factory, an appointment was made for me to interview some of the staff who claimed to have experienced some of these 'happenings'.

On the appointed day, having been given a visitor's lapel badge, I was shown into a side room where I was met by a superintendent, a sergeant, two traffic wardens (one male, one female) and a civilian employee. After introductions, the superintendent took over and everyone related their experiences and although I was allowed to make notes, I was not allowed to take names or record our conversations. All experiences appeared to be genuine and followed the general pattern of what I already knew.

After nearly an hour, I was asked if I would like to go to see where these events had occurred – an invitation only too readily accepted. The sergeant then escorted me through what seemed endless corridors and passages, unlocking and re-locking numerous doors, until we reached one section where I was some feet ahead of him. Suddenly feeling as if I had walked into a cold storage room, I stopped and an awful sensation of oppression came over me.

Turning to the sergeant, I told him what I felt and he said that he was not at all surprised, because this was where even stray dogs being housed refused to pass and often had to be carried. The width of the passage was some 10 to 12 ft and the affected area extended about the same distance, after which everything seemed normal.

A little further on, we came to the traffic wardens' office and, having been introduced, two of the staff related how they had frequently heard footsteps approach the door, then stop, but when they opened it, there was never anyone there, nor did they ever hear the footsteps go away. One obviously very capable lady said that she made sure that she was never left alone in that office, especially on the late shift!

We moved on to the huge underground boiler room, which not only housed several state of the art boilers, but also doubled up as the archives with rack after rack of shelving holding hundreds of files. It was quite easy to understand how people claimed to have seen shadowy figures flitting through the lines of racking; the whole atmosphere seemed somehow depressing and I must admit that a couple of times I found myself glancing round.

While making our way back to the reception area we passed several empty cells – none looking too inviting. I was left in no doubt that having to spend the night there, with the possibility of seeing a phantom or two, would have a distinctly sobering effect!

The Phantom Eyes on Clinghoe Hill

While driving towards Clacton-on-Sea in the very early 1950s, my front seat passenger and I saw something more than a little unusual as we approached the bottom of Clinghoe Hill – this was before it became a dual carriageway – along the A133 about a mile from Colchester.

In the gathering dusk I noticed what appeared to be a pair of large luminous eyes, which seemed to go from right to left across the road and about 4 ft above it, in a weird undulating wavy motion, but thinking that my imagination was running riot, I said nothing.

However, a little later my passenger – actually it was my mother-in-law – asked if I had noticed anything unusual. She confided that she thought she had seen what looked like a pair of eyes floating across the road!

Although both of us were rather baffled, nothing more was said about it until some months later when I was talking with some of my colleagues and the subject of ghosts came up. I recounted the incident, whereupon one of them said that he had heard of a similar incident, which he understood had happened about the same spot. He then went on to say that many years earlier, when he was only a lad, his grandfather had been a groom at Wivenhoe Park (now the site of the University of Essex). He remembered his grandfather telling of the occasion when there had been a big party at the Hall and the guests were leaving quite late at night. Apparently, one of the horse-drawn coaches was making its way down the track – as it was then – at quite a speed and when it neared the bottom of the hill, a herd of deer ran across in front; there was a crash and the coach overturned. Although the occupants were badly shaken but otherwise unhurt and the horses appeared to suffer no ill effects, a number of deer were killed.

It is possible that the large phantom eyes could well be those of the deer, frantic with fright at the impending accident, some sixth sense having told them it would result in their untimely end.

After considerable research, a number of reports came to light indicating that although in the early 1900s a number of ghostly deer had been seen, over the years these apparitions had gradually become fainter and fainter until only heads were visible – and it would appear that even these have now become just a pair of eyes.

The Haunted Red Lion Hotel

One of the oldest inns in Colchester, in fact, probably the oldest, is the Red Lion Hotel, which is in the centre of the High Street of what is also reputedly the oldest recorded garrison town in England. This hotel has been 'home' to many ghosts, both male and female, over the years and maybe this is not so surprising, bearing in mind the age of the building and all the comings and goings; it is also quite possible that some events were tragic.

One such occurrence was in 1633, when Alice Miller was 'fouly done to death' in one of the lofts of the hotel. There are two versions as to why she was murdered. Alice, a young servant girl who 'lived in', became pregnant, but the question was, who was the father – her 'lover' or maybe her own father?

One version of her death suggests that when she became pregnant, her lover, possibly being a so-called 'gentleman' who could either not afford to be involved in a scandal or feared that his wife might find out, led her into what was possibly her sleeping quarters and slit her throat. The other version suggests that she may have become pregnant by her own father and either took her own life, or her father killed her when he found that she was going to have a baby; rather than face the disgrace of being accused of what is now known as incest – let alone having a bastard in the family – he might have decided to take matters in his own hands. However, whichever version is correct, Alice will be long remembered in the Red Lion because there is a bar and restaurant named after her.

Her restless spirit is thought to still wander about the older parts of the hotel and many guests occupying the bedroom beneath the loft where she was said to have been murdered have commented that they have heard vague, indistinct but nevertheless disquieting noises coming from above. Chambermaids often reported hearing their names whispered while working and, thinking they are being called by a colleague, have turned round only to find nobody there. At other times, vacuum cleaners mysteriously switch off and on again while being used, and doors become locked and unlocked even without a key. Other members of staff have alluded to occasions when they were convinced that somebody was watching them while they were working and also a distinct 'chill' in the corridors when this sensation was felt.

Even restaurant staff have claimed to be aware of a presence and some to have even seen a 'white blur' cross the breakfast room when they have been laying the breakfast tables at about seven o'clock in the morning. One day, a young waitress, having gone to the storeroom to get some jams and thinking that there was someone standing close behind her, turned quickly to tell whoever it was – in no uncertain terms – to stop playing about, but found there was no one there. Although it is always cool inside this store, on this particular occasion the temperature seemed to drop considerably.

On numerous occasions it has been noticed, both in winter and summer, that for some unaccountable reason the chandeliers in the restaurant suddenly start to swing gently from side to side, even when all the doors and windows are closed and there is nobody moving about. The room is air-conditioned and there is no possibility of draughts or the central heating causing any turbulence.

An elderly permanent resident claimed to have seen a woman dressed in what he described as 'Stuart costume' standing outside the lounge window, which is on the opposite side of the building to the restaurant, but when he went to speak to her she simply vanished in front of him. Apart from this particular incident he recalled that he had often felt a 'presence' about the place.

A particularly tragic incident occurred in the 1970s when some monks and their party of under-privileged children from London, who were being taken for an outing to Clacton, stayed at the hotel. During the night the new wing in which they were accommodated caught fire and some of the monks and children perished, since when the sound of children in a panic running up and down the corridor has been heard.

There is a sequel to this story, as recounted in 1994 by one of the young waiters. Together with her husband, a lady (who later claimed to have been a practising medium) stayed the night in Room 10, referred to by the staff as 'the haunted room'. Although knowing nothing whatsoever about the history of it, as soon as she entered, she remarked to her husband that she doubted she would be getting much sleep that night because she 'felt' the spirits would be contacting her. The following morning she told her husband that during the night she had been 'contacted' by the apparition of a monk, who introduced himself as Brother Michael and told her that a lighted candle falling over had caused a fire!

It must be emphasised that there was no way this lady could have known anything about the fire or the tragic loss of life. She lived in Nottingham and had never been to Colchester before, let alone the Red Lion. According to the waiter, she promised to write an account for the management, which he ascertained she had done a couple of weeks after her stay.

Even in the kitchen there has been evidence of poltergeist activity; pots and pans have been seen to move of their own volition and on one occasion two of the staff witnessed some of the kitchen utensils rise about a foot above the worktop, hover and then slowly drop back into their original places! One morning, while preparing breakfasts, a cook saw a woman dressed in what appeared to be a greyish-black cloak pass the doorway; she did not see a face, just an outline – however, she realised that she had not heard the very distinctive sound of the kitchen door opening or closing.

Several times chambermaids, having left trolleys loaded with clean bed linen in the corridors, return to find the trolleys gone, only to discover them later in locked unoccupied bedrooms!

One evening, a lady phoned reception and requested a change of room. The receptionist asked if there was a problem, to which the lady replied that her door kept opening and closing of its own accord, despite the fact that she had locked it – but when she tried to unlock it to get out of the room she was unable to open the door. The porter arrived a few minutes later with a passkey, but before inserting the key in the lock, as he knocked on the door, it just swung open.

A now retired porter, who had worked at the Red Lion for many years, recalled a particular wedding reception when, after the wedding breakfast, the bride went to her bedroom to change before taking part in the evening festivities. She was delighted when she opened the bedroom door to find a small table set up with an ice bucket and a bottle of champagne on it and a card 'with the compliments of the management'. Having changed, she locked the door and returned to the party, leaving the champagne untouched. Later that evening, the happy couple returned to their room, only to find the now opened but still full champagne bottle on the dressing table with the two glasses lying on their side beside it and the ice bucket upside down on the bed. Strangely enough, there was no sign of ice, water or even any dampness on the bedclothes but the table was lying on its side in the corner of the room. The whole incident was baffling to say the least!

One evening when the night porter was serving behind the bar and standing with his back to the counter holding a glass up to the optics, he saw in the mirror that his customer suddenly looked round, and at the same time he felt a distinct tap upon his own shoulder. The customer remarked that he had just felt someone push past him, despite the fact that there were only the two of them in the bar. When the porter mentioned the tap on his shoulder, they came to the conclusion that it must have been a ghost!

One afternoon another guest, while sitting by himself in the lounge and just about to turn the page of the newspaper he was reading, was astounded to see a man dressed like a Cavalier pass through the closed door, stride across the lounge and through a window and disappear around the corner leading to the High Street. Apart from these and a few other incidents, everything at the Red Lion Hotel appears to be quite normal.

DEDHAM

The Sweep's Boy

An unusual story was related to me in the mid 1970s by a local man about his daughter, who had lived in a cottage in Brook Street, Dedham until just after the Second World War.

After she and her husband and 5-year-old daughter had been there, very happily, for about six months they began to notice a gradual change in the little girl's behaviour. Formerly a cheerful child, her laughter and smiling face changed to outbreaks of tears and long periods of silence. Obviously worried, they took her to the local doctor for a check up. After a thorough examination he said that although he could find nothing physically amiss, he nevertheless had come to the conclusion that there must be some other reason, possibly psychological, and therefore he would refer her to a specialist.

One day while they were waiting for the appointment with the consultant, the little girl suddenly burst into tears and started screaming for no apparent reason and then without any warning whatsoever ran to the open living-room window and climbed out. The startled mother ran after her and just managed to catch her as she neared the gate and the busy road. With considerable difficulty she managed to drag the kicking and hysterically screaming child back into the house.

Eventually, having calmed her daughter down, the mother tried to find out just what had upset her so much. The child, still sobbing and very weepy between bursts of tears, said it was the boy, the boy with the black face. When pressed for more details about 'the boy', the child explained that she had often seen him in the living-room and he always spoke to her, but today he chased her round the room and when she went to smack him, her hand went right through him and he disappeared!

The mother, realising that her daughter must have seen a ghost, asked the neighbours if any of them were aware of the cottage being haunted. Despite the fact that many of them had lived there for a number of years, none had and as for the possibility of there having been a so-called black child ghost, the suggestion was soon ruled out. Up to that time, there had never been other than white children in the village; in any case, the cottage, so far as they were aware, had always been occupied by elderly people with no children or at least not young ones.

As one might well expect, the story spread around the village like wildfire and it was not long before a very elderly lady who had spent most of her life in the area recalled that many years ago there *had* been a rumour of the cottage being haunted. This information was soon passed to the troubled girl's parents, as a result of which they went to see the old lady.

The following tragic story made good sense to the parents. Many years ago, at the time when chimney sweeps used young boys to climb up the inside of a chimney to clean away the soot, a young boy was suffocated in the living-room flue of the cottage and from time to time it was said that his ghost had been seen in that room – but, strangely enough, only by young children.

Needless to say, with this possible explanation, the house was soon put up for sale and the family moved away. The little girl? Well, she is now a married woman with a family of her own, but wild horses will never drag her to visit Dedham village – let alone the cottage!

The Mystery of Gun Hill House

In the early 1970s, Gun Hill House, Dedham – in the heart of artist John Constable's country – was owned by a Major Green, (retired), and his family. Despite the fact that for some time they had the impression that perhaps the house was haunted, they had never actually seen or heard anything, but nevertheless there was often that weird feeling that they were being watched, especially when they were in the kitchen.

Eventually they contacted me, saying that as they were going away for the weekend they wondered if my son and I would care to spend the Saturday night in the house to see if we could help to solve the mystery.

Arriving about 6 o'clock in the evening and having thoroughly searched the house, checked windows and doors, we made ourselves at home. Apart from the usual creaks one would expect from an old timber-framed house, all was quiet throughout the night.

Daylight came and it was only while making a pot of tea in the kitchen that we both had the feeling that we were being watched. There was nothing evil or malicious about it, just a strange impression that seemed to emanate from near the sink. Despite not seeing anything tangible, we took a number of photographs of the area – more in hope than expectation.

When the film was developed, much to our astonishment we saw that on two of the prints there were white misty columns – apparently coming up from the floor – that we decided could well be columns of psychic energy!

EARLS COLNE

The Haunting of the Coachman Inn

Although the Coachman Inn at Earls Colne is fairly old, it nevertheless has a relatively 'young' history of being haunted. However, having said that much and according to some of its older customers, there may well be a few of the more ancient variety of ghosts gracing the premises, but their appearances have become less frequent in recent years.

In the 1980s a landlord who had only been in residence for a few months related the recent occasion when his son and daughter-in-law, together with their 2½-year-old son, came to stay with them for a few weeks. As was their habit, they put the child to bed in the afternoon in the hope that he would get a couple of hours' sleep and they used an inter-com system in order to hear any sounds from the bedroom. After the first few days they began to hear the child laughing and apparently talking to himself. Thinking that this was something all young children did, the parents were not unduly concerned.

However, one day when his grandmother went upstairs and heard the boy talking, she quietly opened the bedroom door and listened. The child was sitting up in his cot looking towards a corner of the room and still chatting away until he suddenly spotted his grandmother. He stopped speaking and when she asked who he had been talking to, he pointed to the corner and answered, 'That man, who is he?'

She did not tell him that there was no one there, but very carefully asked whether he had seen the man before, to which the boy replied that he always came to visit him and sometimes even played with him! About a week or so later, the young family went home and the grandparents moved into that particular bedroom while their own was being redecorated.

Quickly forgetting about the young child's story, they slept peacefully until one day when, early in the morning, after the grandmother had gone to the window to draw the curtains, she turned and was astonished to see a young man in his early twenties, standing in the corner of the room. He was dressed in a singlet, jeans and trainers and on looking at her a smile came over his handsome young face and then he gradually faded away.

Waking her husband, she reminded him of the story of their grandson and told him what she had just seen. At first he said she must have imagined it; after a while, however, it occurred to him that there might just possibly be something to her story, but he left it at that.

Several months later, a young couple called at the inn and over a drink the young man mentioned that his father used to own the inn and that he had been brought up there as a child. The landlord, remembering his wife's tale, cautiously steered the conversation round and asked if he knew anything about the place being haunted. The youth visibly paled and replied that it was because of the haunting that his father had moved out.

Recovering his composure, the young man then asked what they had seen and where. The landlord related the whole story so far as he knew it and the youth confirmed the sighting of the young man in the bedroom and went on to explain that the figure that had materialised was in fact *his* brother who had been killed in a motorcycle accident just outside the inn and that particular bedroom had been his. Naturally the family had been devastated at the loss of their eldest son and it was only shortly after the accident that his apparition started to appear in his old room and down the stairway. This, of course, had proved far too much for the family; they sold up and moved away, hoping that perhaps time would help them get over their tragic loss.

FRINTON-ON-SEA

The Haunted Radio Station

At the time of which I am writing, i.e. the 1980s/1990s, the once exclusive Essex seaside resort of Frinton-on-Sea, or as the local residents preferred to say 'inside the gates', had only one main access to and from the Colchester to Walton-on-the-Naze main road and that was via the railway crossing, the gates of which therefore virtually controlled all access into the town, the railway running parallel to the main road for some distance.

Radio Mellow 1557, north-east Essex's local radio station, was in a building alongside the main road 'outside the gates', and according to those who worked there, they were convinced that it was haunted by a very solid-looking male ghost.

One day a presenter was standing at the end of a passage not normally open to visitors because it led to studios 'A' and 'B', which were in constant use, when he saw somebody pass along the far end and enter studio 'B'. He was surprised, and not a little annoyed, because he was due to use that particular studio within a matter of minutes and he was not aware that he was to share it with anyone or even record an interview.

More than a little curious, he went along the passage and on reaching the door and looking through the glass observation panel, to his amazement he saw somebody bending over the console, sitting in what should have been *his* chair! What was even more intriguing was the fact that the red light that would indicate the studio was in use was not switched on. However, being a professional presenter, he would not enter while someone was in there, despite the absence of the red light.

He went back to the end of the passage where he had been waiting for a female colleague to join him. When she eventually arrived and he told her what he had seen, she said that she too was unaware of any change in plans and walked down the passage to see for herself, only to find that not only was the studio empty, but that it was abnormally cold!

It was then that the local Psychical Research Group became involved and a considerable amount of background investigation was carried out. It became clear that long before the building became a radio station, it had been an old house, which in the course of time had been considerably enlarged, and studio 'B' was in part of what was the original building. After further research, it was discovered that many years earlier there had been a murder in the house, which was apparently linked to a dispute between a group of smugglers who operated from the Ship Inn at nearby Kirby-le-Soken and, it is thought, the owner of the house.

GREAT BROMLEY

Strange Happenings at Seven Rivers

The Seven Rivers Cheshire Home in Great Bromley, near Colchester, is just one of a number of convalescent homes founded after the Second World War by Group Captain Leonard Cheshire VC, specialising in the care, general well-being and rehabilitation of people with physical disability. Many of the patients are so incapacitated that they are unable to move even their limbs and have to totally rely upon the staff for their every need. One such patient, with great difficulty and in the presence of two members of the nursing staff, managed to relate a very strange event that he experienced at Seven Rivers early in 1993.

Being completely disabled, he was only able to move his lower jaw, but by a rocking movement could alter the position of his head a fraction of an inch at a time. One evening he was put to bed as usual, lying on his back with an alarm, which was plugged into a socket in the wall behind him, placed near his head so that in an emergency he could activate it. Sometime during the night, he became aware of an unseen force carefully lifting him bodily up and over the high-sided guardrail of his bed, which of course had been routinely raised by the nursing staff. He was then very gently lowered to the floor and covered with a blanket.

The whole sequence of events was carried out with such care that even the ultra sensitive facial alarm was not disturbed. Had the power supply been interrupted, the alarm would have sounded automatically. When the nursing staff made their routine inspection during the night, they were horrified to find their patient sound asleep *on the floor*!

This mystery was never solved and possibly never will be; after all, how was it possible for him to have been lifted and lowered to the floor without activating such a sensitive alarm? Not to mention the fact that it normally took three highly trained nurses to lift him. Also, why should any known or unknown force do such a thing? Could it possibly have been for some form of psychic healing?

What a pity that perhaps the answer will never be revealed, if indeed there is an answer. So far as can be ascertained, there is no history of psychic activity or psychic healing having taken place there before or since!

GREAT CLACTON

St John's Church

Apart from the mysteries and intrigues of St John's church and churchyard in Great Clacton about which I write of below, the building has a special place in my heart because it was here that on 22nd November 1947 I married the girl who was to be my wife for the next 52 years.

The Mystery of the Gravestone
Beneath a tree in the churchyard is a slate headstone that records a particularly tragic incident at sea, just off the nearby Essex coast on the infamous Gunfleet Sands.

The inscription on the headstone reads: 'In loving memory. Rice Parry, the beloved son of John & Sarah Parry, of Bangor, North Wales. Born September 28th 1873. Perished at sea tied to the rigging of ship "J.W. Babel" of Beaumaris. Which was wrecked on Gund Fleet Sands 10th March 1891.'

At first, one might be forgiven for wondering, apart from the tragedy of it all, what is so special about this. Well, in the late 1980s, a group of students were given a school project to carry out on churchyards in the area. About eight of the group elected to visit St John's and make the churchyard with its table vaults and gravestones the centre of their studies.

One young lady, having spotted the only slate headstone among several stone and marble headstones, was immediately attracted to it. After reading the inscription, she realised this was not only something out of the ordinary, but also something she could follow up by going to the local library and hopefully discovering more about what had obviously been a horrifying event. Apart from making a rough sketch, she also made a copy of the inscription but, strangely enough, what she made note of was not the inscription above, but one relating to a young *girl* who had lost her life while tied up on a boat!

When she handed in her work, her teacher noticed the similarity to some of the other essays – except that the others referred a *boy* who had lost his life. Gathering the class together after the last lesson, she asked for an explanation and they all insisted they had copied the inscription correctly! Being a Friday, the teacher suggested that during the weekend they should individually go back to the churchyard, double-check their facts and rewrite their essays as a part of their homework.

When on the following Monday morning the teacher read their various accounts, it was with almost utter disbelief. The student who had previously noted that it was a *girl* who had lost her life now admitted that she must have been mistaken; when re-reading the inscription she saw that it referred to a boy. However, two boys now found that they were wrong in saying that it was a boy who had lost his life – they now insisted that the inscription clearly showed that it was a girl!

A few years later, a young local housewife who was interested in reading some of the unusual inscriptions on gravestones, chanced to see this slate headstone and stopped to read the inscription. She noted that it told of a girl who had been tied to the rigging. Later that night, she told her husband what she had read and remarked how sad it was for a young girl to have died in such dreadful circumstances. Her husband, recalling the story of the headstone from his own schooldays and thinking that perhaps this must be the very same gravestone that had caused so much controversy at school years ago, suggested that they go to the churchyard together the next evening to check the wording.

To the young lady's surprise, they found the inscription did indeed state that it was a *boy* who was drowned – but she too was still prepared to swear that the day before it clearly stated that it was a girl who had perished! According to historical records it was Rice Parry who lost his life on the ship *J.W. Babel*. The mystery still remains – how is it possible that so many people appear to have misread the wording when the inscription is incised so clearly?

Another Churchyard Mystery

Late one Saturday afternoon in September 1993, a lady living in Burrs Road, Great Clacton was returning home after doing her weekend shopping. Because her bags were very heavy, she decided to take a short cut along the footpath that goes through St John's churchyard.

She was just passing the front of the church when her attention was drawn to a young lad aged about 9 or 10 years running about the churchyard, but when he saw her looking at him, he ran off in the direction of Puffinsdale. The more she thought about him, the more she wondered about how a 10-year-old could possibly run that fast and, another thing – nowadays, most boys of that age would be wearing jeans, whereas he appeared to be wearing a pair of shorts coming down just below his knees.

There is a sequel to this story told by another lady who was not only quite unaware of the above occurrence, but did not even know the lady involved.

On a bitterly cold morning in November 1993 (approximately nine weeks after the above story) this lady – also returning home with her shopping and walking through the churchyard – was about halfway along the path when she too saw a young boy aged about 9 or 10 years, apparently playing among the gravestones. Her attention first drawn to him by his antics around the headstones, but she then noticed what she considered to be his rather old-fashioned, late 1800s or early 1900s clothes – a pair of knickerbockers down to his knees, a rough cloth shirt and a pair of braces.

Her first thought was, fancy a mother letting a boy dressed like that go out to play in this weather. Without thinking, she started to walk towards him, but as soon as she got within some 10 ft of him – he just vanished!

One Sunday early in July 2008, Ron Bowers from Holland-on-Sea visited the church after having heard the unusual story from a friend concerning the experiences of the two ladies. Ron – an amateur photographer – having his camera with him, took a number of pictures of what he was convinced was an empty churchyard, but when he later examined them, one showed an unexplained mist in front of a tree, while another clearly showed what appears to be a child surrounded by vapour! One can only wonder if this possible spectral child was the same one seen by the ladies 15 years before.

It would be interesting to know if anyone else has seen what surely must have been an apparition of a child or if any reader has information about his history.

The Haunted Clock

Sometime during the 1980s a lady related this strange story about her husband's uncle who had lived in the now demolished Blacksmith's Cottage at Aingers Green. He had been one of the last village blacksmiths and whenever she and her husband went to visit him at the cottage, they noticed that he had a habit of getting up every few minutes and poking the fire with a very large iron poker, which they knew he had made himself.

Some years later, when he had died and the cottage was being cleared, her husband was asked if there were anything he would like as a memento and he chose the poker and an old bakelite-cased clock that had always stood on the mantelpiece, both of little monetary but of considerable sentimental value.

Taking them home to their bungalow in Great Clacton, he put the poker against a heavy brass fender in their lounge and the clock on the tiled surround. A few nights later, they were both awakened by the unmistakable sound of the fire being poked, followed by what sounded like a poker rolling across the tiled hearth.

Hastily rushing out of bed and into the lounge, they switched on the light, half expecting to see their young daughter playing with the poker, only to find that not only was there no one in the room, but the poker was in its usual place on the fender. They then checked their daughter's bedroom – the girl was fast asleep!

The following night when the same sounds were again heard and as before there was nothing to account for the noise, they became really worried and, after a short discussion, decided that the apparently offending poker should be put into the garden shed.

However, never be too complacent! All was quiet for the next few nights and they were congratulating themselves upon having solved the problem, when once again they heard the same noise, now followed by a thump, thump as if the poker were being used to break a large lump of coal. A couple of minutes later, the clock, which had not been wound since they had inherited it, suddenly started to chime, but in a weird and eerie way.

There was only one thing to do – consign the clock to the shed to join the poker. However, for some unaccountable reason, after it had been in the shed for over a year her husband decided to give it a clean and if possible get it working properly. When it had been stripped, cleaned, oiled and reassembled, he left it on a shelf in the kitchen in order to later adjust the timing. That night, once again, the sound of a rolling poker followed by the same thud, thud, thud came from the lounge, soon followed by the chiming of the clock.

The following morning the clock was unceremoniously dumped back into the shed, the couple having come to the conclusion that it must be haunted by the blacksmith's spirit and there was no way that they were prepared to have it in the bungalow.

A particularly strange thing about the whole episode was the fact that the fireplace in the lounge was not an open coal-burning fire, but a gas fire, set in a tiled surround.

A few weeks later, the lady wrote to me and a visit was arranged. I spent a very interesting evening listening to versions of the story from both the husband and his wife and 'inspecting' the fireplace, clock and poker but found nothing unusual to account for the disturbances. I was just about to leave when they offered to give me the clock – an opportunity far too good to miss – and I took it home and put it on a shelf in my own garage.

There was a strange sequel to this story. A couple of weeks later, having been booked to give a talk on the paranormal at the Officers' Club in Colchester Barracks and thinking that this story, being fresh in my mind, would make an ideal finale, I took the clock with me. Putting it on the table with its face towards the audience, I carried on with my discourse, intending the talk to finish at about ten o'clock. Dead on the hour the clock started to chime, struck ten and, on exactly the last stroke, a bottle of wine that had been on a table a couple of feet away suddenly exploded. Had it been stage-managed, it couldn't have been timed better, much to the delight of at least a hundred sceptical army officers!

There was one more intriguing thing about the clock. I did not have a key that fitted it and to the best of my knowledge it had not been wound up since I'd had it – and I certainly hadn't set the time!

The Rocking Chair and the Invisible Barrier

In Great Clacton, there was, until the early 1980s, a row of thatched cottages on the corner of Burrs and Valley roads that were reputed to be the oldest remaining still-occupied cottages in the area. Although many people were of the opinion that they should have been preserved for posterity, unfortunately they were demolished to make way for a new housing development.

However, quite a few years before they were pulled down, one of the tenants had two rather unnerving experiences. She was a lady in her twenties, and one day she was sitting in a rocking chair in her front room with her young child in her arms, gently rocking backwards and forwards when, to her horror, the chair slowly lifted into the air and remained about a foot from the floor, still rocking.

Recovering from the initial shock, she jumped down and, with the child still in her arms, ran towards the back door. It was then that she received her second shock; before she could reach it, she met with what she later described as an 'invisible barrier'. Whatever it was, it seemed to bar her way and she was unable to get past it, no matter how much she tried. Getting more frantic by the second, she turned and headed past the chair – still suspended in mid-air and still gently rocking – until she got to the front door, through which she went without any further trouble.

As she ran into the road, her screams for help were soon answered by one of her neighbours who, after listening to her very disjointed story, went back into the house with her – where he found everything to be normal. The chair was on the floor and they were able to walk quite freely through to the back door.

The lady concerned, now quite elderly, who related this story to me, was prepared to swear that every word was the truth!

Just why this strange phenomenon should have taken place remains a mystery, there being no record of anything remotely like it having happened at the cottage before or after.

GREAT DUNMOW

A Haunting in High Street

Without any hesitation whatsoever, in the 1980s when a recently married woman was offered the chance to rent a first floor flat in a 17th-century building in High Street, Great Dunmow, she readily agreed. Not only would it be their first home, but as it was only a short distance from the inn where she worked as a barmaid, often late at night, its position was a great advantage. However, she was quite unaware that the building was haunted and the first indication she had of this was when she went to sweep out the flat in readiness for the carpet layers.

Arriving about half an hour before they were due, she tidied up and stood the broom in a corner against the wall. The men arrived on time and, having brought in rolls of carpet, they spotted a couple of nails protruding from the floorboards. They produced a hammer to tap them down, but in doing so brought up a lot of dust from between the joints in the boards. One of the men asked if he could borrow her broom, but before she could answer, the broom literally flew across the room towards her. The carpet layers, hardly able to believe what they were seeing, finished the job in double quick time!

When the couple eventually moved in, things were quite normal until after a few weeks they began to hear heavy footsteps late at night in the corridor outside their flat. At first they ignored it, but when the same thing happened night after night, the husband decided to find out who it was. When he heard the steps approaching, he flung open the door, at which not only did the sound stop but to his utter surprise, there was nobody there and nothing to account for the noise.

There were numerous occasions when the husband would go to meet his wife from work and, as they walked along the street, they would see lights on in their flat and rush up the stairs, only to find the place in darkness. At other times their lights would be switched off while they were in the flat and although they clearly heard the click of the switch, before they could reach it, the lights would go on again, with another definite click!

From time to time they heard not only tappings but also more distinctive knockings that defied explanation, particularly when they knew they were the only occupants in the building. After some months, they finally decided that enough was far more than enough and moved elsewhere.

GREAT HOLLAND

The Headless Coffin Bearers

A young man – well known to me – whose grandfather had at one time lived in Pork Lane, Great Holland, near Clacton-on-Sea, related the following story which his father had told him and he had no reason whatsoever to believe it to be other than the absolute truth.

His grandfather, a farm labourer, was working on the top of a threshing machine with sheaves of wheat being thrown up to him at a steady pace for him to feed into the machine. Something causing a slight blockage made him take his eye off a sheaf that was already on its way up and it caught him off balance and, with pitchfork in hand, he was knocked from the machine and fell to the ground, injuring his back.

In the 1930s there was no such thing as the National Health Service and unless you subscribed to a 'penny a week' doctor's club, you had to pay for everything, including emergencies, and with the farm workers' pay so low, few could afford even that.

However, while the poor man lay on the ground obviously in great pain, the local midwife happened by sheer good luck to cycle past and one of his fellow labourers called her to have a look to see if she could do anything to help him. Naturally she readily agreed and soon said that he had badly damaged his back and there was little anyone could do to help him other than to get him home and put him to bed.

His workmates gently lifted him onto a hurdle and, having carried him home, carefully took him up the stairs and put him to bed. His wife produced a half bottle of whisky, some of which he quickly drank to help deaden the pain.

Later that evening, while the family were in the living room discussing the accident, they heard him scream suddenly and, dashing up the stairs, they were astonished to find him out of bed and standing by the window, holding the curtains with one hand and pointing out into the darkness with the other. He was talking excitedly, apparently oblivious of his pain, and gesticulating across to the cornfield beside the railway.

Straining their eyes towards what he was so desperately trying to show them, they saw six men carrying a coffin on their shoulders along a path that many, many years ago had led to the cemetery – and all appeared to be *headless*!

With great difficulty the family put him back into bed and, having given him more whisky, left him to sleep. The next morning they found him dead.

GREAT HORKESLEY

A Very, Very Strange Case

Although many stories tend to end with a tragedy, this actually started with one. In the early 1980s, tragedy struck a couple who had been married for some years – the wife sadly took her own life. For six or so years, the grief-stricken husband continued to live by himself, until he eventually met a lady who in time became his wife and they started their life together in the husband's house.

At first all went well, until unexplained things began to happen. Various items, such as keys and money, would disappear – sometimes to reappear only a few days later in unlikely places, while at other times they would be missing for months on end. Rather than trying to blame some mischievous spirit, the couple put the losses down to their own absentmindedness.

After a while, however, mysterious red stains appeared on the walls by the stairs and no matter how often they were washed off, within a few days they reappeared, even after the walls had been sealed and re-wallpapered. When the couple's dog took to standing at the bottom of the stairs, with its hackles up, barking at something invisible, only to back away whimpering, they started to be more than a little worried.

Later – witnessed by several people – wedding photographs hanging on the walls would swing from side to side and one of the strangest things of all was when a jug full of gravy disappeared, only to be found some time later in the deep-freeze! Nothing unusual in that perhaps, until it was realised that the jug was lying on its side with the gravy frozen horizontally and none had run out despite the fact there was no cap or lid.

In July 1995 a new phenomenon started – involving their toothbrushes, which were in a glass over the washbasin in the bathroom. While his new wife's remained untouched, the man's became distorted on several occasions.

In August the same year, a new pair of scissors vanished and a few days later the husband opened the boot of his car, only to find them on the floor. When he attempted to pick them up he realised that they were red hot! Retrieving them with a pair of long-nosed pliers, he laid them on the ground until they cooled down, and it was only then he noticed that the steel had 'blued' with the heat, despite the fact that they were brand new and so far as he knew had never been used.

At this point the couple decided to call for help and contacted the Ghost Club Society. Two investigators agreed to carry out a preliminary investigation, followed by a visit by a 'rescue' medium. Without being given any information – apart from the name and address and the fact that help had been requested – he arrived 'cold'.

As soon as he entered the house he was able to make contact with an entity and also identify it, but at that moment the new wife arrived home (she had been out shopping when he arrived) and the contact was broken. The medium found he was unable to restore it while the lady was in the house, and an appointment was made for a further visit.

During September 1995, after arrangements had been made for the lady to be away, the medium visited for a second time. Having established contact with the entity, he suggested a possible line of action to alleviate the problem. At first this was thought to have been successful, but after a few days a new line of 'attack' was initiated by the spirit – medications began to disappear from the medicine cabinet in the bathroom, only to reappear in other parts of the house, again witnessed by other people.

During October the same year, a new phenomenon occurred when the front of a clock, which normally stood on the mantelpiece, would fly open and the whole of its 'works' crash onto the hearth. It was not until the clock had been repaired several times that it was realised that this occurred only when a woman either entered the room or phoned the house. This phenomenon was witnessed by at least three independent witnesses!

On 18th October 1995, a new toothbrush (the seventh) became distorted after being used only once. All the toothbrushes were kept as evidence. Eventually, everything became far too much for the couple; they put the house up for sale and moved away from the area, So far as is known, there has been no further trouble in the house and no disturbances have been reported from the couple at their new address.

The general conclusion by those involved in this investigation was that the spirit of the lady who committed suicide while in an unstable state of mind (she had been a Staff Nurse at the local mental hospital and this was possibly caused through her work) was earth-bound and for some reason she wanted to attract her husband's attention. Perhaps, when he remarried, she could not accept the idea of another woman living in *her* house with *her* husband, but when the couple moved away, her problem was resolved and the disturbances ceased.

GREAT WALTHAM

Hauntings at the Beehive

When a new landlord and his family moved into the Beehive public house at Great Waltham, near Chelmsford, in the early 1990s, the 'regulars' turned out in force to welcome them, doubtless hoping to enjoy a customary free pint on the house. In the course of the evening and amid much light-hearted banter, some of them related a number of stories about the pub being haunted, which the landlord took in good part, thinking that this was their way of welcoming him or at the worst 'winding him up'.

However, as time passed, he and his wife began to wonder whether they were victims of their customers' jokes – or was the house actually haunted? Morning after morning, the toilets at each end of the pub would smell strongly of cigar smoke and some mornings there would be quite a thick haze at one end in particular, but despite keeping a watch for any regular cigar smoker in the bars, they saw nothing.

Being a bit of a sleuth, the landlord became so intrigued that he decided to delve into the history of the pub and paid a visit to the Essex Records Office where they produced details going back many years. It soon became apparent that a part of what was now the pub was built on the site of a former saddle-maker's workshop; it was reported that his wife, who died in childbirth, was in the habit of smoking strong cigars!

One morning at about 8.50 am a cleaner ran out of the lounge bar screaming and repeating over and over again, 'It didn't open the door, it didn't open the door.' When she eventually calmed down and was asked what it was that didn't open the door, she said that she had seen a white cloud-like object come out of the wall, cross the bar and pass through the door, without opening it. If it had actually opened the door, perhaps she would not have had the sort of shock that necessitated her being off work for a couple of weeks!

On yet another occasion, when the landlord's wife was going up the stairs, a grey cat shot out of the private lounge and disappeared *through* the bathroom wall. Although she could hardly believe what she was certain she had seen, she felt that if she told anyone, they would think that she was mad. So she kept it to herself, but from then on, every time she went up those stairs she kept a wary eye out for the cat.

About six or seven months later, she saw it again – a grey cat – go straight out of the upstairs lounge and through the bathroom wall in exactly the same place. She still dared not tell anyone, however!

A year or so later, she was in the bedroom when she heard her husband, who was coming up the stairs, suddenly say 'Bloody Hell' several times. She rushed out onto the landing and called out 'What's up?' to which he replied, 'You will never guess what I have just seen' – and it became obvious that the cat had appeared again.

Occasionally, the landlord's brother-in-law – who hated cats and the animals naturally sensed it – came to stay with them and slept on a camp bed in the upstairs lounge. On numerous occasions he complained that he had been woken up during the night by a cat walking over him, but when he switched on the lights, there was no sign of one. Knowing all too well his intense dislike for cats, they always took the precaution of making sure that their own pet was locked out, so there was no way it could have been theirs!

About a year or so after the cat on the stairs incidents, the landlord's wife was asked to go to a tarot card session and, despite being somewhat sceptical, she went. The man reading the cards apparently saw something that he was reluctant to tell her but, when pressed, he eventually revealed it was to do with a cat that had been killed for a bet of some kind, but the disturbing thing about it was that 'should she see the cat again it would be a disaster'. He then went on to say that tarot cards would sometimes warn of things that *could* happen and therefore enable you to be on your guard.

One evening the landlord, while organising an outside catering engagement, left his wife to run the Beehive where, at closing time, she followed the usual practice of taking out the till drawer and carrying it upstairs to put it into the safe. As she was about to climb the stairs, such a weird feeling came over her that she went back and sat in the kitchen for over two hours, until her husband came home. To this day she is convinced that had she gone up those stairs, she would have seen the phantom cat and a disaster of some kind would have happened and no one would have found her for over two hours. Strangely enough, they never saw the cat again!

Handed down over the years, there is a story that when the Beehive was rebuilt some time ago, an Elizabethan ghost known as 'Old Ruffy' moved in. Who he really was, nobody is sure, but he was reputed to cause glasses to disintegrate, mainly during the night but occasionally while actually being held in a customer's hand!

A regular customer, having read about 'Old Ruffy' in a book, made a note of the details in order to tell the landlord at the time and his family. He was reading the account out aloud in the bar one night, when suddenly there was a loud crash in the kitchen. The landlord and as many as nine customers rushed in to investigate the noise. Although there was no one in the kitchen, one of the chairs, the sort with horizontal rungs at the back of it, had literally fallen apart and the rungs were in an orderly line about 6 ft away across the floor on the far side of the room.

Obviously, 'Old Ruffy' did not like his tricks being read out aloud in the bar. After this evening, however, the landlord and his wife accepted the fact that 'Old Ruffy' was trying to draw attention to himself and they would often talk to him, especially when a lot of 'little incidents' occurred, as they did from time to time.

HARLOW

Poltergeist Activity at The Hornbeams

In 1977 three elderly ladies, having been friends for many years, decided to pool their resources and share one of the newly converted apartments in what had once been a very large house known as The Hornbeams in Harlow; the property obviously taking its name from the large number of these magnificent trees in its grounds.

The ladies had only been in residence for a few weeks when they were plagued by what turned out to be a fairly violent male poltergeist. Over the next eight or so months, he regularly terrorised them in one way or another, at times just moving objects around in their rooms, at others hiding things away and a few days later returning them to their original places. Sometimes he would awaken them during the night by clumping around their bedrooms as if wearing hobnailed boots; in fact, it was almost as if he were conducting a personal vendetta against them.

On one occasion, he was apparently in a particularly aggressive mood because after stamping around one of the bedrooms, he suddenly stopped, lifted up the bed on one side and tipped out the now screaming lady before letting the bed crash back to the floor with an almighty bang!

When, according to another of the ladies, he actually made one of his rare manifestations, he gradually appeared as a 'blazing ball of white fire that just seemed to hover and, as it floated towards you, you could feel it touch you – it was like a numbing chill.'

Eventually, the ladies were unable to stand the situation any longer – either they or 'it' would have to go. They chose the latter and called in a priest who agreed to perform a service of exorcism, which much to their relief and eternal gratitude appeared to have been successful because they were no longer troubled by their unwelcome visitor.

As a postscript, I later discovered that one of the former occupiers of The Hornbeams, having been jilted by the lady he was to have married, became so distressed and mentally unbalanced that he became a confirmed woman-hater and eventually took his own life in the house.

HARWICH

The Electricians' Shock

The following story was related within a few days of the actual incident by one of the electricians involved and when I interviewed him later his story was confirmed by the affected carpenter. Both were prepared to swear that every word was the absolute truth.

In 1962 two electricians, when working for the Eastern Electricity Board, were instructed to replace the main electric cable from the road to the meter in the cellar of one of the Georgian houses close to the old Treadmill Crane at Harwich.

Quite apart from these two electricians in the cellar, other tradesmen – carpenters and painters – were busy on the upper floors. It was normal for them all to leave coats, boots and lunch bags in the cellar, and the sole entrance to this was from the hallway, the front door being some 3 to 4 ft above ground level and reached by five steps.

One morning, when the electricians were working in the cellar, a carpenter arrived and, after hanging his lunch bag on a hook on the wall, he changed his boots for a lighter pair of shoes, in order not to risk any damage to the polished floors, and then went upstairs.

The electricians were only concerned with their own problems and apart from the usual banter about him being a 'part timer', they didn't take too much notice of the man or his bag – until a few minutes later when they both saw the bag lift from the hook and slowly float across the cellar and loop itself over another hook on the opposite wall. Not believing what they had seen, the braver of the two went over to the bag and lifted it off the hook; having examined it, he put it back on the original hook.

Lunchtime came and the electricians went outside to their van to brew a very welcome pot of tea. No sooner had they settled down than their peace was shattered by an almighty scream from the direction of the house – followed by the carpenter falling headlong down the steps outside the front door.

Naturally rushing to help, they found him shaking, apparently with fright, and muttering unintelligibly. After they had helped him back to their van and calmed him down, he haltingly told them what had frightened him so much. He said that when he went to the cellar for his lunch bag and put his hand up to get it, it literally jumped off the hook and flew around the cellar at head height at very high speed, just missing him by inches. He dashed for the door with the bag whirling round and round close behind him – the rest they had seen for themselves!

Leaving him sitting in the van to recover, they continued with their work in the cellar where everything was calm and normal. Not only was the carpenter's lunch bag never seen again, but the carpenter – not surprisingly – never returned to the house either!

After I had heard this story, I tried to find out something of the background of the house, but apart from the fact that on at least two occasions exorcisms had been carried out, I drew a blank. The owner, a retired solicitor, stated that he had no wish for any further investigation to be conducted during his lifetime; he was fully aware of the situation but had no inclination to discuss the matter!

KIRBY CROSS

Horseshoe Cottage

As a result of a request for an investigation into unaccountable 'happenings' at Horseshoe Cottage, Turpins Lane, Kirby Cross, near Frinton-on-Sea, I paid my first visit on 15th July 1996. The occupants were Gary and Karen Emberson and their three children – Jamie, aged 10, Jade and Kelly. The cottage, which was detached, was built in 1975 on land that had previously been part of a fruit farm and was next to two semi-detached cottages used to house retired servants from the farmhouse.

The Embersons had moved into Horseshoe Cottage in August 1994 and Karen explained that it was only a day later that Gary noticed a lady, dressed in red, walk across the bottom of their garden. The same lady was also seen, on another occasion, by a visiting relative.

On the day of the first sighting, a picture entitled *The Three Judges* fell from a shelf, breaking its glass. Later an ornamental owl suddenly 'flew' from another shelf and crashed to the floor some feet away; later still, a glass-topped table suddenly shattered!

Two days prior to my visit – 13th July – a chandelier hanging from a heavy 2-inch hook in the lounge ceiling was considerably damaged when it crashed to the floor.

The eldest child, Jamie, absolutely refused to sleep in his bedroom, insisting that he heard not only footsteps on the stairs but also noises like an engine being revved up, sometimes sounding like a motorbike and on other occasions like a car.

Karen related that after moving in they had a string of bad luck; their car was badly damaged in an accident, the brakes on their van failed, nearly causing another accident, and something stored in the loft suddenly fell through the bedroom ceiling, among other worrying incidents.

Apparently a previous tenant told Karen that they had noticed 'strange things' from time to time, but had refused to elaborate. Further investigation revealed that earlier occupiers had lived there for four years when the lady had suddenly dropped dead in the kitchen and her husband died a few days later in hospital.

My next visit was on 7th August and while I was sitting in the kitchen with Karen and Gary discussing the events referred on the previous visit, we were joined by Jamie – obviously a very worried boy – who badly wanted to talk about *his* experiences. He said that it was usually at about five o'clock in the afternoon that he heard what sounded like a car or motorbike revving up, ending with the noise of glass smashing as if in a crash. When asked if this first started when they moved into the house about two years earlier, his reply was somewhat startling – he said that even when they lived in 44 Coopers

Lane in Clacton the same thing happened. After a break, we all went up to Jamie's bedroom, where a distinct humming sound was apparently coming from his bed. This seemed to increase as we went closer, only to stop suddenly. At this point we were joined by a lady investigator, who suggested that she should leave her crucifix on the boy's table and say: 'In the name of the Father, the Son and the Holy Spirit, depart in peace.' No sooner had she said these words than there was a noticeable quietness, followed by a distinct feeling of peace.

We all went into Jade and Kelly's room where everything seemed normal, before moving into Karen and Gary's bedroom where we noticed a 'cold spot' near the window, but nothing oppressive. As we were leaving the room, I heard a soft voice say 'They need not worry', after which we went downstairs into the hall, where again we all felt a 'cold spot', but this time it was *very* cold. Moving into the lounge there was yet another 'cold spot', which extended across from an armchair to a sofa and appeared to exude a most unfriendly atmosphere. This seemed to be mainly directed at me and gave me a tight feeling at the back of my neck, causing a headache. Thinking that perhaps this was because I was standing beneath where the chandelier had been, I had a strong feeling that we all should leave – which we did.

My next visit – accompanied by a psychic medium – was on 23rd August. As soon as we entered the cottage the medium said that her guide was telling her that all was now clear and well, but that Gary and Karen should move as soon as possible.

Just before Christmas the same year, I made a further visit on the off chance, but a neighbour said that the family had moved out a few weeks earlier – without leaving their new address!

LAWFORD

The Mysterious Church Choir

It was 1940 – wartime – and as happened so often all over the country, a young lady had gone to the railway station to wave goodbye to her soldier boyfriend after he had spent far too short a leave. She started to walk sadly back to her home in the village of Lawford.

Although it was after 10.30 at night and dark, the moonlight was sufficient for her to see her way along the footpath through the fields. She had no fear about taking this short cut home although it went through the village churchyard and past the church, which had a reputation for its 'strange happenings'. However, as she approached it, she saw that it was fully lit despite the fact that there was a strict blackout in force. Thinking that the caretaker must have forgotten to put up the shutters, she drew nearer and heard the choir singing. She knew for certain that the local choir had been disbanded 'for the duration' and yet here was a fully lit church with a choir singing at 11 o'clock at night!

Now becoming concerned that something was obviously very wrong, she went to the south door of the church and tried the handle, only to find it locked. At the same moment she realised that not only had the singing stopped, but also the lights had gone out. She waited for a few minutes, fully expecting people to emerge, but when nobody appeared she became frightened and ran home.

The following day she went back to the church and, seeing the caretaker, told him what had happened. All *he* could say was that there was no way any lights could have been on in the church, because the power had been disconnected owing to the wartime restrictions, and regarding the singing, there had been no choir – as she knew only too well – since the outbreak of war!

LAYER MARNEY

The Haunting of the Virgin Mary's Church

Immediately behind Layer Marney Tower and in the shadow of its lofty Gate House is the village church dedicated to the Virgin Mary.

One Easter in the 1900s, while Helen Shaftsbury, a promising local artist, was sketching the beautiful St Christopher painting that hangs in the church, she distinctly heard a rustling behind her followed by a soft voice saying 'Marney'. When she looked round, there was nobody to be seen and although she knew quite well that it was not her imagination, she nevertheless carried on sketching. However, when a few minutes later she again heard the same sound followed by a much deeper voice saying 'Marney', she got up and walked about the church, looking for anywhere anyone might possibly be hiding, but still found that she was quite alone.

About ten minutes later, it happened for the third time and, feeling not a little exasperated, she jumped up and called out, 'Who's there? What do you want?' Although there was no response, her attention was drawn to the monument bearing the inscription 'Sir Henry, FIRST LORD MARNEY'.

Enough was enough, she packed up her drawings and left. Later when she met the vicar and told him what had happened, he said that several other parishioners had also heard a voice calling out 'Marney', and on most occasions it had been around Easter or early May – the anniversary of Sir Henry's death. Strangely enough, every time the voice had been heard, the person hearing it had been looking at the St Christopher painting!

The vicar also told her that his predecessor had actually seen what he was convinced was the wraith of Sir Henry apparently walking down the chancel, away from the painting. He also said that he knew of at least two other people who claimed to have actually seen the ghost, but that was in the nearby Layer Marney Tower.

Early during the 1990s Mrs Sheila Charrington, who owns the estate together with her husband Nicholas, told me a strange story. A few Christmases earlier, they had invited a few house-guests for the holiday period and, as was their usual practice on the Christmas morning, they walked along the private path through the churchyard from the tower to the church. To the surprise of all of them, they saw what could best be described as a spectral headless chicken running about between the gravestones, only to vanish as suddenly as it had appeared!

LEIGH-ON-SEA

The Haunted Bank House

The following account was written in the early 1990s by the lady who then owned The Bank House, Leigh-on-Sea.

'Ridiculously big. Why do you need all these rooms? How are you going to do it up?' Friends threw a lot of stick at me when I bought it because the house had a weird feeling about it. Dark, musty, low ceilinged, partially ruined by having been partitioned off into flats by previous landlords, ancient wiring etc – but I fell in love with it and, in my imagination, I was Jane Eyre living in Thornfield Hall, the only thing missing – Mr Rochester!

Having been built in 1751 it was a daunting task, nevertheless, within six years, not only had beams been exposed, but it had been re-wired, re-plumbed and renovated to some of its former glory. When artist John Constable visited his former nanny, who at one time lived there, it was where he allegedly did the sketches for his famous *Hadleigh Castle* during his stay.

The huge music room, built later on the back of the building, was awe-inspiring, with an inglenook fireplace and a 22 ft high Tudor beamed ceiling and stained glass inset into the huge bay windows, and was where author Dennis Wheatley held several meetings.

One night (or possibly early morning) I needed the bathroom. The dim half-light cast gloom across the black and white Italian marble floor in the foyer of what was after all originally a bank and the swing doors – with gold leafed cupids set above them – had been pulled back to allow some airflow, the humid night being the aftermath of a very hot summer's day.

I stepped onto the ice-cold marble tiles; the coldness made me alert and as I walked through the swing doors and up the stairs – the top of which was obscured by the ceiling of the hall – I saw something move above me. There, on the landing at the top of the stairs, was a woman dressed in a diaphanous dark blue muslin gown that looked old and threadbare. She glided into the room that overlooked the garden where usually the view of the sea and the moon competed for beauty.

Instinctively I knew that what I had seen was not human and I had to reluctantly admit to myself (a sceptic) that I had seen a ghost. Being naturally nosy, I crept up the stairs, anxious to see more. I stood in the room but there was only blackness; there was no moon that night and being in the middle of re-wiring this particular room had no lights either.

'Is there anybody there?' I called. What was I doing, hoping for an answer? If I wanted a sign that my eyes hadn't deceived me, I was to be denied. For some minutes I stood waiting, every hair on my body alive and tingling. Wide-awake and disappointed, I eventually went downstairs to bed, but there was no sleep.

When, later, I laughingly told the story to an old resident of Leigh, I half expected to be dismissed as crazy; instead I got a shock and was very relieved when I was told, 'Oh, dark blue muslin she was dressed in? Then you must have seen the old lady of Leigh. Usually she wanders round the library gardens.'

LITTLE CLACTON

The Ghostly Birthday Reminder

The following story was told me by a lady from Little Clacton, who freely admitted that although she had never really believed in the existence of ghosts, just in case there were such things, she was at least prepared to keep an open mind on the subject.

One afternoon, she was sitting in her lounge playing the organ; she loved music and was a reserve organist for two local churches and spent most of her spare time rehearsing a full repertoire of hymns and voluntaries. However, on this particular day, while really enjoying herself playing all her old favourites, she became aware of a very strong feeling that she was being watched.

Knowing full well that she was quite alone in the house, she shrugged her shoulders and carried on playing. However, as time passed and the feeling became more intense, she stopped playing and swung around on her stool. To her utter astonishment, sitting in an armchair and obviously enjoying the music, there was the apparently solid apparition of her *late* next-door neighbour who had died some six months previously.

Prior to his death, it had been his habit to call round in the afternoons when he knew she would be practising and just sit quietly in that armchair, thoroughly enjoying the music until he dropped off to sleep, and many times she had jokingly said, 'One day you will die in that chair!'

On this particular day, those words – said in jest – came back to her, but by the time she recovered from the shock, the apparition had faded away. With her mind racing, she began to wonder if his appearance was intended to bring a message or even a possible warning of some event to come. It suddenly dawned on her that the next day would be 30th June, his widow's birthday and she had forgotten to buy the bunch of flowers or even the birthday card that she had promised him she would get every birthday to show that he was still thinking of his wife!

She rushed out, not only to get a bunch of flowers but also *two* cards from the village shop and, upon her return, offered a silent prayer to her friend and good neighbour for his timely reminder.

Tales from the Mortuary

During the 1980s, a part of what used to be Springfield Garage in Little Clacton had been a mortuary and Chapel of Rest used by a local undertaker. Although this was a few years back, for some time afterwards there were reports of strange 'happenings' that, rightly or wrongly, were blamed on the days when the bodies of the deceased were kept there pending burial or cremation.

One particular incident stood out in the minds of all those who saw it. This was when a mechanic in the garage, having been carrying out some welding work on a car, finished his job, turned off the gas taps on the burner and laid it on the concrete floor to cool off. As he walked away, he had taken only about four paces, when he heard something move behind him and, looking round, saw the gas burner rise about 3 ft from the floor, ignite and head towards him – flame first.

Showing great presence of mind, he rushed over to the cylinders and turned off the gas supply but, although the flame died out, the heavy brass burner still chased him. Not stopping to ask any questions, he ran out of the garage and had only reached the forecourt when there was an almighty crash from inside where he had been working. Later, it was found that this had been caused by the trolley and the two heavy gas cylinders that were chained to it; they had fallen over and been dragged some 6 ft across the floor.

On another occasion, one of the other mechanics was drilling out a broken stud on a wheel hub when the bulb in his lead light exploded. There was nothing particularly unusual in that, but as he was returning with a new bulb, he was surprised to hear his electric drill start up. Passing from behind the car on which he had been working – to say that he was astonished would be a gross understatement – he saw his heavy drill 'hovering' about 3 ft from the ground as if being held by some invisible hand. This was far too much for him – he turned tail and ran!

Meanwhile, strange unaccountable things happened in the shop and storeroom. Boxes were moved around, stock disappeared only to reappear a few days later, strange noises, moans and groans were frequently heard, yet apart from the fact that it was once a mortuary there was nothing to account for this phenomenon!

Haunted Holland Road

The following account was given to me in 1991 by the young lady involved, just a few days after she encountered what she could only think was a ghost, in Holland Road in Little Clacton.

At about 9.30 pm she was driving – accompanied by her fiancé – from Great Holland to her home in Little Clacton. Having just rounded a sharp bend and crossed over a railway bridge, they suddenly ran into a patch of mist. Slowing down, she leaned forward to switch off the car radio, when her fiancé shouted out there was a man on the road. She braked hard, but before she could stop, the figure seemed to be halfway across the bonnet.

Although he appeared to be solid, neither of them felt or heard anything of the impact. However, they both noticed a sudden icy feeling as who or whatever it was apparently passed *through* the car.

Unable to see any sign of the man or any damage, they cautiously continued their journey, both fully convinced they had seen a ghost.

MARKS TEY

The Silver Elephant

In May 1991 a gentleman from Marks Tey related a story that by any standard is truly remarkable. If one calls it a coincidence, then it must surely rate as being a many million to one chance – or was it?

It all started in 1987, when a middle-aged gentleman who had been living and working in India for a number of years unexpectedly returned home to England after having been advised by his doctor that he had an incurable disease and his life expectancy was somewhat limited. Having come to terms with the situation and determined to make the best of his remaining years, he decided that it would only be right that, having been abroad for so long, he should spend his remaining days with his family in England.

Although by no means wealthy, he nevertheless felt that he should bring something back from India that would always remind him of where he had been happy but at the same time be an acceptable gift to his family.

After searching around for some time trying to find something suitable, he happened to stop to watch a silversmith at work in a bazaar. The Indian craftsman was working on a set of three silver elephants – a large bull, a smaller cow and its calf. He was immediately attracted to them and after the usual haggling over the price, a deal was struck. Ten days later, when they had been completed, assayed and his initials and the date had been engraved upon each of them, he was able to collect them.

On his arrival in England, a small family gathering and a 'welcome home' party was held, during which he proudly presented his mother with the gift of the elephants with a request that they should remain in the family forever. They were immediately given pride of place on the sideboard where they were greatly admired by all.

Later that evening, the celebrations having finished, he, his mother – a widow – and his brother were sitting quietly in the lounge talking over old times and generally reminiscing and, as it seemed the ideal opportunity to tell them of his medical condition, he explained his reason for coming back much earlier than expected. After the initial shock the conversation began to evolve around illness, mortality and the possibility of life after death. On the latter point, after much discussion and still certainly not being fully convinced that there actually *was* life in the hereafter, they came to an agreement that whoever passed over first would, if possible, give an unmistakable sign to those remaining.

In due course he passed away and his mother and brother, remembering their conversation, anxiously waited for the promised sign.

Some time later, the house was broken into and among the items stolen were the three silver elephants. This was a particularly severe blow, not only because they were so highly treasured, especially by the mother, because they were the last gift from her departed son, but to lose them in such a manner was nearly far too much for her.

A few weeks later, although the police recovered two of the elephants – the bull and the calf – there was no sign of the cow. When the two pieces were eventually placed back on the sideboard there was a feeling of emptiness; they just did not look or even feel right without the other one.

About a year later, the mother died and the remaining son was left to tidy up the family affairs, which entailed a visit to a solicitor in Ipswich whose office was over an antique dealer's shop. He arrived at lunchtime and, finding the office closed and with time to spare, his attention was drawn to the antique shop – not that he was particularly interested in antiques, but somehow he felt compelled to look into the window. To his utter surprise, in the centre of a display there was a silver elephant. As he later admitted, he trembled because he was absolutely certain that it was the stolen elephant, which meant so much to him.

To his dismay, the door was locked but while standing there just looking in the window and hoping that the proprietor would soon return, he saw the solicitor's staff return and disappear up the stairs.

Hoping and praying nobody would come along and buy the elephant, he apologised to the receptionist saying that it was imperative that he was dealt with as soon as possible and, having signed several papers, he made a hasty exit, nearly colliding with an elderly lady. Murmuring an apology, he dashed into the street and was relieved to see a man who he took to be the owner, just opening the door.

With a quick glance in the window, just to make sure that the elephant was still there, he went into the shop. Wasting no time, he asked to see it. As soon as it touched his hands, he was certain that it was the one and, looking underneath, there sure enough were his brother's initials. Without even thinking about any legal implications, he asked the price and said he would take it. While parcelling it up, the antique dealer remarked how lucky he was to get such a beautiful item, because it had only been brought into the shop that morning and he had placed it in the window just before he went to lunch!

One can only wonder whether or not it was just coincidence, or was it the long awaited sign of the possibility that there is life after all – perhaps in a different dimension – in what we call the hereafter?

MISTLEY

The Sandeman Port Ghost

It has often been said that all good stories should begin with 'Once upon a time', whether they be fictional or true – so there is no reason why *this* true story should be an exception, although in this case 'Once upon a time' was actually Christmas Eve 1956.

My wife and I had been invited to spend Christmas with some relatives at their old farmhouse in the little village of Mucking, situated on the very edge of the Essex marshes, just a few miles from the town of Grays. The farmhouse was only approachable by a single lane that crossed the main Southend to London railway by means of a level crossing, the gates of which were operated by a gatekeeper.

That year, Christmas Eve fell mid-week, which meant that most of the twenty or so guests who were to spend a few days at the farmhouse and had probably been at work would be arriving during the evening. Not only was it very cold and there had been a slight fall of snow, but the heavy, dark clouds threatened more to come. However, inside the farmhouse it was far from cold; the huge inglenook fireplace with seats on either side of the blazing log fire was giving off that lovely aroma of burning wood and, at times, that of the odd apple log. There were two enormous hams in their muslins hanging from large hooks in the chimney, just as in earlier days.

The lounge with its ceiling and walls well covered with Christmas decorations was lit only by old fashioned oil lamps and the flickering flames from the log fire helped to show off to perfection the Christmas tree in the corner with its tiny candles appearing to give off little halos. The fairy doll, perched on the uppermost branch, waved her wand over heaps of gaily decorated parcels stacked around the base of the tree.

In the adjoining dining room, not only was the long refectory table already laid up in preparation for a meal but there was a sideboard loaded with bowls of fruit, nuts and sweets. Yet another sideboard had been converted to form a bar, its top covered with bottles and glasses of all kinds, certainly enough to cater for everyone's taste.

The walls were draped with Christmas cards on strings, and the ceiling with its old oak beams was festooned with balloons, holly with masses of red and yellow berries and, of course, ample strategically placed sprigs of mistletoe. The whole scene was set for what was surely going to be a perfect Christmas.

By late evening all the guests had arrived, supper had been served and eaten, drink was flowing freely and everyone was really entering into the spirit of Christmas. It was inevitable that the topic of conversation should eventually get around to the subject of ghosts – what better time, place and setting could there be for a good ghost story!

After we had listened to several spine-chilling tales and personal experiences, the old, old question arose – were there actually such things as ghosts, was it all in the mind or was it just a cover for something else? Some of the guests had their doubts, but others were well and truly convinced that they really did exist in one form or another. Although they admitted that they had never actually seen a ghost, they said they would certainly be delighted to have the experience, even if only to prove a point!

The host, having had a busy evening making sure that everyone had been settled in, now said that he could tell us about something that had happened to him and that those present who had known him over the years would be aware that he was truthful, level-headed and even, one might say, fearless.

His story went back to the early 1940s, when he was the bailiff of a farm in Bradfield, near Manningtree. One winter's night he and his wife went to a dance in Manningtree and as it was wartime there was no petrol available for such luxuries as attending dances, so they had to use their bicycles. On that particular evening, having thoroughly enjoyed themselves and while making their way homewards in brilliant moonlight, they soon came to a small hill where they were able to freewheel down the slope at a good speed. About halfway down, set back from the road was a large old farmhouse that was partially obscured by a clump of trees, which extended from the house to the edge of the road.

As they approached the trees, they saw a tall man standing on the opposite side of the road, just beyond the trees. In the bright moonlight they could clearly see that he was dressed in a long black cloak with a tall wide-brimmed hat – similar to the advertisement for Sandeman port. He was then joined by a much smaller person – also dressed in black – after which they both started to cross the road in front of the cyclists as if completely oblivious of them. Our host, being slightly ahead of his wife, swerved to avoid them, at the same time shouting out, not only to warn his wife but also to curse the couple for their stupidity.

His wife, however, *had* seen them, but despite quickly braking she was travelling too fast to avoid running into them – but instead of crashing into what had appeared to be two normal solid human beings, she careered right through them. When she realised what had happened, she wobbled and fell off her cycle. In the meantime, her husband, having stopped and dismounted, looked back just in time to see his wife pass straight through the figures, who carried on walking as if nothing had happened and disappeared into the thick hedge!

Our host, always a very good storyteller, really excelled himself in his description of what happened and, of course, telling it from first-hand experience made it sound even more exciting.

At this point, everyone was sitting with bated breath, all so intensely interested that they were actually living through the experience themselves, when all of a sudden, there was a heavy rapping on one of the windows, causing, without exception, everyone's heart to miss a beat. It was the gatekeeper from the level crossing calling to say that it was nearly midnight and, as he was going off duty, did anyone wish to use the crossing before he closed the road and locked the gates for the night!

The Sequel

More than ten years passed and I had given very little more thought to that Christmas ghost story, when, out of the blue, two middle-aged men from Clacton who worked for me in my building business, related a strange experience *they* had had along that same stretch of road while on their way home after working in Manningtree.

Their story was particularly interesting inasmuch as it was basically similar. They were travelling home together in a car driven by Dave and as they descended the small hill near the old farmhouse, George, the passenger, suddenly shouted out, 'Stop Dave, for Christ's sake, you've hit him.' Dave skidded to a halt and, turning to George, said, 'What the hell are you talking about?' or words to that effect, using his natural Cockney vernacular! George replied, 'That man – didn't you see him, he walked right in front of us, we hit him for sure.'

They both hastily got out of the car, but could see no sign of anybody lying in the road. When they walked back to the spot where George thought he first saw the man, there was nothing to be seen and there were no marks in the tall grass beside the road where anyone might have walked or crawled. They returned to the car and when they examined the front of it, there were no dents, no broken headlight glass, nothing to indicate an accident of any kind.

Back in the car, they talked over what had happened – or at least what George was convinced had happened. He was positive that he had seen a fairly tall man wearing a long black raincoat and what he took to be a sou'wester hat, standing by the trees on the opposite side of the road; as they came down the hill, the man had walked in front of them and there was no way they could have avoided him! Dave was sceptical. After all, he had not seen a thing and there was no bump and definitely no body! 'No, George,' he said, 'either you fell off to sleep and dreamt it, or you saw a ghost.' George was adamant that he had not fallen asleep and was equally positive that he *had* seen the man. Agreeing to differ, they continued their journey home to Clacton.

However, even this was not to be the end of the story. The following morning when they called in the office and knowing of my interest in the occult, they could hardly wait to tell me their story. It brought back memories of that Christmas all those years ago. It was too much of a coincidence; there was no way they could have possibly known on my relative's experience. This clearly called for a spot of research and for the next few months I spent a considerable amount of time making enquiries around the area.

After apparently getting nowhere, I struck lucky one day when an elderly lady, who had lived in the area all her life, vaguely remembered that when she was very young her father, a farm labourer, told her never to go near the old farmhouse because it was haunted. When she became a teenager and asked her father to tell her about the farmhouse and why it was supposed to be haunted, he related the following story.

Many years earlier, what was then a farmhouse had, in fact, been a small mansion owned by a wealthy wool merchant. It would appear that he had a beautiful teenage daughter who was having a serious love affair with a groom from nearby Mistley Hall, an association of which her father so strongly disapproved that he forbade her to see him again. However, they still continued with their nightly assignations in the shadows of the clump of trees on the hill. One evening her father, returning home earlier than usual, spotted the lovers together and later that night he told her that this was going to be her last warning and if they did not stop seeing each other, he would take matters into his own hands. He tried reasoning with her, explaining that not only was the groom of a lower class than her, but there was also good reason to believe that he was already married with children.

This final warning obviously had little or no effect and the clandestine meetings continued until the young couple eventually decided that, rather than be parted, they would run away together. The girl's father was very suspicious and kept a wary eye on her and it was not long before he realised what they had in mind. Night after night he laid in wait by the trees for the groom to appear. One night his patience was rewarded, a figure crossed the road and headed for the trees where it disappeared from view.

Not to be thwarted at this stage, the father edged his way through the trees until, in the faint moonlight, he saw a figure silhouetted beside a large tree. He raised a blunderbuss to his shoulder, took aim and fired, not realising that his dearly beloved daughter was in her lover's arms and consequently they both died.

Could this be the real explanation for the phantom figures crossing the road – a spectral re-enactment of a terrible tragedy?

UNNAMED ESSEX HOSPITAL

The Consultant's Letter

The following account was the subject of a letter I received in June 2003 and the reader will fully appreciate that, although the location of both the hospital and the name of the consultant have been withheld, there is little doubt that it is true.

In his letter the consultant said that about ten years previously while working in an Essex hospital, he fell into conversation with a theatre sister called Mary, a true professional, who described to him how one night, around 1 am, when she was alone and managing the crash theatre, another nurse came through the doors almost in a state of panic. Mary recognised her as a nurse who she was under the impression was a patient in another ward, but the other nurse told her that she had been discharged and was now back at work. She said that there had been an emergency call asking for the theatre to be readied for a car crash victim, and then went to prepare the equipment.

When Mary checked the status of the emergency call, she was told there was no such requirement, and on phoning another ward she learnt that her nurse visitor had in fact died some four hours earlier. She went back to the theatre and although there was no sign of the other nurse the equipment had been fully readied. What Mary could not understand was that there was no way out of the theatre except past her and it was while she was pondering this that a call came in asking for the emergency theatre to be readied for a 12-year-old child with head trauma – just as Mary's visitor had said.

Probably helped by the fact that there was a prepared theatre, the child survived and Mary was in no doubt that she had conversed with and had been assisted by a ghost nurse. She had no reason to make this up and the consultant was absolutely convinced it really occurred!

WESTCLIFF-ON-SEA

The Haunted Studio

When, in 1929, three young ex-art students decided to open an art studio and school, they found a flat over a café in London Road, Westcliff-on-Sea that suited their purpose. Elsie, who had been an actress, producer and writer, gave drama lessons, while Leslie taught music and used his talent as a pianist and music arranger to good effect. The third member of the trio was an artist who, between commissions for sketching and painting portraits, also taught the basic skills to a number of aspiring artists. Each had their own room, and there was also a larger one they used for group activities.

One day while the three of them were sitting in the kitchen discussing their own particular part of the business, Elsie suddenly gave a stifled scream and, pushing her chair violently to one side, cried out, 'Did you see it? It was horrible and it got hold of my leg.' After being calmed down, she described what had so terrified her. She said it was a most unpleasant creature: a pale, thin young man, about twenty years of age and unshaven, with untidy sandy-coloured hair. She then went on to add that he had suddenly appeared, and when she screamed he ran out of the room.

Strangely enough, the only one to have seen anything was Elsie, a very steady and down-to-earth young lady, who swore that she would never be able to forget the sight and touch of him, let alone the imbecilic expression on his face.

When they checked with the estate agent to see if he knew of anything unusual about the building – such as the possibility of it being haunted – he admitted that he was aware that there had been talk of hauntings in the past, but because he did not believe in such things, he had disregarded it! However, he did recall that at one time an elderly couple with a mentally deficient son had occupied the rooms.

Later, the proprietor of the café below said that while renting the rooms as an extension to his business, he had received complaints about a lad who would try to force his unwelcome attention on the waitresses. Eventually the café owner decided to confine his business to the ground floor.

Apparently the lad, very much an imbecile, had died of tuberculosis and the parents had moved out only a few months before the three ex-art students had taken over the rooms.

Shortly after Elsie's experience, the spectral visits became more frequent, until eventually they became almost daily, but after their conversation with the estate agent and now being aware of the tragic situation – although still somewhat apprehensive – they were no longer afraid and became determined they would not be driven out by a ghost!

Some time later when Leslie was going down the stairs carrying a notice board that he intended to stand outside, he dropped the board and ran back upstairs shouting, 'The blasted thing touched me, it rubbed itself against me and pushed me against the wall.'

A few days later, while the artist was hanging some paintings on the wall of his studio, he became aware of a misty shape close to him and, on turning round, he saw the 'fog' resolve into a wavering human figure, which sprang backwards as though alarmed. The artist, although somewhat shaken but with considerable presence of mind, managed to speak to the 'shape', saying that there was no need to be afraid, nobody would hurt it. At the sound of his voice, the figure retreated and seemed to feel its way around the walls until it came to the open door, through which it vanished.

Later, when he told the others what had happened, they came to the conclusion that the poor soul was obviously too mentally sick to understand that physically he was dead. He didn't know how to dematerialise and believed that he still had to leave the room by the door! The general opinion was that the extremely low mentality of his physical counterpart had prevented him from understanding the true state of affairs.

A few days later, the three of them were once again in the kitchen, just as they had been at the time of Elsie's first experience, when they all clearly saw the entity – exactly as Elsie had earlier described it. Once again, apparently when it realised that it had been spotted, it appeared to slink away through the open door. The three of them talked over the various options of how to rid themselves of this obviously tormented spirit. Exorcism was ruled out as being too drastic, but one thing was for certain, they had to find a way to keep it away from Elsie. She was obviously its target because it seemed to be persistently pursuing her and she was now becoming more scared and horrified at its every approach.

They finally decided that they should try to concentrate upon it jointly and bathe it in an imaginary white light in the hope that if they combined their thoughts in sympathy rather than enmity, it would then realise that they were trying to help!

This seemed to bring about a rapid improvement. The 'ghost', if such it was, began to show an ever-decreasing fear of them and the molesting of Elsie stopped almost immediately. For a few days it would just appear and stand looking at her, but not attempting to touch, until gradually it seemed that it had learned how to dematerialise and was no longer dependent on making its exit through open doors.

After some months, what had at one time been a two or three times a day appearance, gradually became only occasional until eventually, after a single red rose mysteriously appeared one morning on Elsie's typewriter, 'Ben', as by then he had been nicknamed, was never seen again. The studio somehow never again felt complete without him and all three were left wondering if it really was their 'thought power' that had helped him on his way!

WICKHAM BISHOPS

Maybe There *Is* Something in Ghosthunting!

Some years ago I gave a talk on BBC Radio Essex on 'Ghosts and Hauntings'. The presenter, who incidentally, although quite a sceptic, was at least prepared to 'listen and learn', found that I had raised a few points that had mystified him. He threw out a challenge (on air) to take him, together with a recording engineer, out one night on an investigation.

Knowing only too well that this could well prove risky and that little or nothing might happen – apart from a severe loss of pride on my part – I reluctantly agreed that I would contact him in due course. In a 'damage limitation' effort, I took great pains to explain that ghosts, poltergeists or any other phenomena do not appear to order and he might well have a wasted night. With a wry grin, he said he accepted the point but if nothing happened on that occasion, he would still like to come again sometime in the future.

A few weeks later, an all-night vigil was arranged at a derelict church in Wickham Bishops, which had been deconsecrated for over two hundred years. At one time it had been in what was the centre of the village, which for some reason was moved about two miles away to higher ground, leaving the church isolated and decaying.

The surrounding graveyard still contains many graves with headstones and also a few vaults, many of which have been vandalised, as has the interior of the building. The whole area is now overgrown and neglected, but over the years there have been numerous reports of '*things*' having been seen and heard, including several accounts of a ghostly figure apparently hanging from a tree with its head on one side as if its neck were broken. There have also been unconfirmed reports of what would appear to be a piano accompaniment to a choir singing hymns, coming from within the church.

There have also been stories of vague figures seen gliding from grave to grave, accounts not taken too seriously because, strangely enough, the least haunted place – contrary to belief – is a churchyard. Nevertheless they cannot be completely disregarded, any more than can the pinpricks of light seen darting about both the graveyard and inside the remains of the church itself.

It seemed an ideal setting to which to invite the radio presenter and his sound engineer. A time and date were agreed and arrangements made with a team of experienced investigators to be there also. The November night selected turned out to be cold, crisp, clear and moonlit, with a slight breeze, just enough to move the branches of the trees and bushes to add atmosphere, as if any were needed.

The team assembled at 9 pm, leaving their cars beside the road and carrying their equipment some 400 yards along a cart track to the site. After a brief meeting, allocating positions to cover as many angles as possible and arranging for partner changes every hour on the hour, we set off to our allocated places.

The radio presenter and his colleague had a roving commission to visit every position and record an interview with anyone they wished. All was quiet for about three long, cold hours, during which a few pinpricks of light were reported, but nothing major. At about 2 am, just as a change of positions was due, a report came over our radio link that something strange seemed to be happening near the boundary where a fence used to be; it was the sound of a no longer existing gate opening and closing on creaking rusty hinges, followed by a distinct click of a latch. This occurred four times within half an hour and was recorded on two occasions.

Just after 3 am a thick mist came down, making the church look even more eerie. Because the cold was becoming almost unbearable despite us all wearing thick overcoats, gloves and hats, it was then decided to go into the remains of the church for a little shelter and to drink the rest of our coffee, also to have a conference on the night's results, while the radiomen could conduct their last interviews by the light of about a dozen flickering candles.

Without any warning, we all heard a loud creaking sound and a sound as if light footsteps were climbing a flight of stairs, followed a few minutes later by the noise of them coming down again. During the sudden hush that followed, while all that could be heard was the radio engineer quietly carrying on with an interview, there was a loud click and his recorder stopped dead. It was found that the batteries had gone completely flat despite the fact that they were brand new and would normally have lasted at least another ten to twelve hours.

To sum it all up, although the night was not as eventful as we had all hoped, it was not without its moments and our Radio Essex men had to admit that maybe there is something in ghosthunting after all!

According to a report in 2001, it was understood that planning permission had been granted to convert the old church into a holiday home and by 2003 it had become a very fine house.